I0752832

J.W.Lincoln Del.

G.G.Smith & J.W.Watts Sc.

FIRST BAPTIST MEETING HOUSE, PROVIDENCE, R.I.

ERECTED A.D.1775.

Joseph Brown. } Architects.
James Sumner.

AN ACCOUNT

OF THE

CHURCHES IN RHODE-ISLAND.

PRESENTED AT AN ADJOURNED SESSION OF THE

TWENTY-EIGHTH ANNUAL MEETING

OF THE

RHODE-ISLAND

BAPTIST STATE CONVENTION,

PROVIDENCE, NOVEMBER 8, 1853.

BY HENRY JACKSON,

PASTOR OF THE CENTRAL BAPTIST CHURCH, NEWPORT, R. I.

PROVIDENCE:
GEORGE H. WHITNEY.
1854.

INTRODUCTION.

The following pages contain the Report presented by Rev. Henry Jackson, Vice President of the Rhode-Island Baptist State Convention, at an adjourned meeting of the Twenty-eighth Annual Session, held in the Meeting House of the High Street Baptist Church, Providence, Nov. 8th, 1853.

The following Resolution was adopted at the Annual Meeting, June 23d, viz:

"*Resolved*, That the Rev. Henry Jackson, Vice President of the Convention, be requested to make a tour through the entire State, visiting all the Churches connected with the Baptist Denomination, and collecting such information as may in his judgment be deemed advisable, to report at an adjourned meeting of the Convention in the ensuing Autumn."

The Report, after having been read, was by the Convention referred to a Committee of six, to make such disposition of it as they in their judgment should deem proper. The Committee at their meeting on the 21st of November, after due deliberation, directed that it should be published for the use of the churches, and requested the author to furnish them a copy for the press.

In this Report the author has been obliged to rely very much upon the returns of the United States Census of 1850, as found in the office of the Secretary of Rhode Island. On this account, and also because he was unable to make himself acquainted with the statistics of the various Denominations from personal interviews, some inaccuracies may exist, especially as since that time changes have occurred—still he has endeavored as far as his opportunities have allowed him, to present the number of the churches and the places of public worship in Rhode-Island, as they existed in January, 1854.

REPORT.

MEMBERS OF THE RHODE-ISLAND BAPTIST STATE CONVENTION:—

RHODE-ISLAND, although geographically covering an area of only 1340 square miles, and embracing 857.000 acres, has nevertheless gained for herself great honor and renown; and she is abundantly worthy of all the cultivation which we have in our power to bestow upon her. In his kind providence, a providence all wise and just, God gave to our ancestors this soil, and the privilege to administer in its waters, for the first time in America, Christian Baptism to believers in Christ, on the profession of their faith in Him, as taught in the New Testament and practised by our Lord and his disciples. And it was also granted to them to give to the world in the simplest and most distinct form, liberty of conscience and illustrations of its exercise. The Charter of this Colony, obtained from Charles II, July 8th, 1663, through the agency of John Clark, then in England, was the first *full legal* instrument that the world ever saw, wherein the rights of conscience in all matters of religious faith were guaranteed to every citizen alike, and in which no one was required to submit to any legal restraint, except in civil affairs alone: a charter, the priviliges of which had been shadowed forth in the convictions and sentiments as expressed by our fathers from the earliest settlement of the Colony, as well as in the principles of the charter previously obtained from the Earl of Warwick by Roger Williams, (who was specially commissioned for the purpose,) bearing date March 17th, 1643–4; but they were concentrated in this more ample instrument, the main feature of which is so prominent in the Constitutions of our own day, and they were adopted and proclaimed as a law in this State, January 23d, 1843. This high praise was awarded by the talented Callender to "Mr. R. Williams and Mr. J. Clark," when he remarked, that these "two fathers of this Colony, appear among the first who publicly avowed that Jesus Christ is King in his own kingdom, and that no others had authority over his subjects, in the affairs of conscience and eternal salvation." In its application to Mr. Clark no one has refused to acknowledge the correctness of this declaration; and certainly from Mr. Williams no one has any just ground to withhold it. For so strenuous was the latter for religious liberty, that he would not allow that any human power had any right even to grant it, much less to curtail it; and hence he carefully avoided any reference to it in his charter, making mention therein only of *civil* freedom, which was all he desired from a human court, and which, as he contended, was all that any such court had any just right to legalize; the great Judge and Creator having granted to man as an inalienable right, the liberty to worship Him as every one chooses to elect, provided he offend not against the public peace.

The guarantee of this liberty, as well as its conception, we as Baptists claim; and it is a matter of devout gratitude that as such we have never held any adverse opinion ; nor have we at any time ever persecuted another sect on account of the religious sentiments they propagated; nor on any other ground have we sought to bind their consciences. And it remains for us in our measure to fulfil the high trust committed to us equally as to our fathers, that the link binding the present to the past be not broken, and that this doctrine by our means fail not of regenerating the race. And my prayer is, that the Author of liberty and the God of Peace, will in his abounding grace, grant to men of every nation that same freedom of thought and conscience in religious things, which was in the beginning, is now, and as I hope ever will be, so entirely untrammelled and unrestrained in this same Rhode-Island. Not but that the institutions of religion should be protected and even sustained by statute law as they at present are, but that no one should be compelled to worship God in any manner, or to attend upon any form of worship whatever.

My visit to the Churches I commenced soon after your annual meeting. The greater portion of them I met in their own sanctuaries, and with the condition of all I have made myself acquainted. With an account of these I enter upon this report. My remarks will embrace the number and pecuniary resources of the churches of all denominations in the State, but will especially describe those of our own body, which I denominate in their collective capacity, THE RHODE-ISLAND BAPTIST STATE PASTORATE, including every interest that now exists, or that may hereafter be formed in connexion with the ASSOCIATED BAPTISTS OF THE STATE.

By this designation I would not awaken the jealousy of a single member, for no one can he more tenacious than myself, of the independency and sovereign right of every church to govern itself according to the gospel of Christ, it being the judge of the requirements and the priviliges thereof in its individual capacity as a church, and being accountable alone to the great Head of the church, asking at the hand of the civil tribunal simply a protection in the free enjoyment of its religious convictions in due subserviency to the laws of a sound civil and judicial government.

Roger Williams was educated under the direction of Sir Edward Coke, to the legal profession, but subsequently he became first an Episcopalian and then a Congregational minister, having left the former to obtain in the latter denomination greater liberty of conscience. Having left England in the pursuit of the same purpose, on his arrival in Boston, February 5th, 1631, he met with strong opposition to the sentiments that he had fondly cherished in his native land, and which first drove him to Salem, and thence to Plymouth, and finally banished him after his return to Salem from the Massachusetts jurisdiction. This man, thus sentenced, in order to escape from a condition so unjust, secretly left his house and wandered amid Winter's perils to Seekonk, and thence, when yet pursued, to our shore, (June 1636) then a wilderness occupied by the natives of the forest; and because he had reached a spot where the Boston Court could not control him, he called the place PROVIDENCE in honor of his God, like the patriarch of faith, when upon his deliverance he beheld the offering, saying, "*The Lord will provide.*" This was the man who, at the age of thirty-two years, sought a home in America, because, as he had learned, he could there have one "of piety and freedom;" and who, after a singular experiment in the country of his choice, stood when thirty seven years old, on a territory mainly the gift of Indian affection, and who there advocated "entire and unrestricted religious freedom," and that the civil magistrate had no right "to deal in matters of conscience and religion." And this was the man who, from his first landing in Massachusetts, cared for the Indian, and feared not when in banishment, to enter his domain, relying upon his protection; and who, as long as he lived, was as celebrated for his love to the dwellers in the woods, as for his defence of civil and religious freedom, unrestricted to all who love and maintain the true principles of law and order.

Having become convinced of believer's baptism, he viewed himself unbaptized, and became, not an Ana, but a Bible, Baptist. He therefore sought this ordinance, and by appointment of the eleven disciples then united in an holy band, he was baptized in March 1638–9 by Ezekiel Holliman ("a poor man," it has been said, but not poorer than his master,) and thus on that day was witnessed the first New-Testament baptism in America, so far as records show, or tradition reports; and to which occasion we trace the rise of our Denomination in the New World.

I write of Roger Williams, the first missionary to the natives of our soil and the "first legislator in the world," (at least in its latter ages,) "who fully and effectually provided for and established a full, free, and absolute liberty of conscience." "He was," as Gov. Hopkins affirmed, "the first to maintain this doctrine," as his charter abundantly confirms, for, as has been remarked, he most cautiously avoided asking for any thing that he believed the king had no power to grant; society in his estimation requiring no other laws than those that secure to the community good and just order, and to its members the peaceable enjoyment of their individual opinions, so far as they do not interfere with the exercise of the civil compact. And, that I do not write unadvisedly concerning Mr. Williams' views of religious liberty, is confirmed by the concluding sentences of the code, which contains like his charter nothing except civil regulations. This code, which was adopted at the meeting of the first General Assembly, reads as follows, "otherwise than this, which is herein forbidden, all men may walk as their consciences persuade them, every one in the name of his God. And let the lambs of the Most High walk, in this Colony, without molestation, in the name of Jehovah, their God, forever and ever." "This noble principle," as Knowles has said, "was thus established, as one of its fundamental laws, at the first Assembly under the charter. It is indigenous to the Rhode-Island soil, and is the glory of the State." At that meeting of the Assembly no man was more efficient than Mr. Williams, who with his charter then in hand rejoiced that nothing had been done to militate against his own sentiments, or those of his charter.

But in these opinions and sympathies Mr. Williams had many co-operators. There was John Clark, a physician and a preacher, who, beholding the spirit of the Boston Court in 1637, (being then twenty-eight years old,) proposed to his friends "for peace sake, and to enjoy the freedom of their consciences," to remove beyond its jurisdiction. This proposition was received by them with unanimous approbation, and he with some few others, went into New Hampshire, seeking a cooler climate, but on account of the great severity of the winter did not long abide there, but determined to go South, and on their return left their vessel to pass the cape, while they came by land to the settlement of Williams. Between this man and Williams there was then formed a friendship that never was broken. It was with Mr. Clark that Mr. Williams so heartily engaged in the purchase of Aquetneck, called in 1644, Rhode Island, from the Indian Sachems, Canonicus, and his nephew Myantonymy. And this was that legislator also, who framed the code of laws for the subsequent government of the Island, and as these laws virtually constituted the basis of the laws of the Colonies when united under the name of "Rhode Island and Providence Plantations," it is supposed that he to a great extent was the author of that system of government which was prepared in Newport by some one whose name was not announced, and which was adopted at the meeting at Portsmouth, May 19th, 1647.

And Mr. Clark,—with Mr. Williams, fully deserves all the eulogy with which either of their names has been honored. And it is delighful also to contemplate these two apostles of liberty, inseparable in their mutual attachment, and undivided in their services. To the one was granted to obtain the first charter under the seal of the Earl of Warwick, March 17th, 1643–4; and to the other, the second charter of July 8th, 1663; and to both was given a joint embassy to England, in 1652–3, to procure the reversion of a commission granted to one of the Islanders, by which the first charter was impaired. By their united efforts the said reversion was obtained, so that the government was continued as under the first until the second charter of Clark; a charter, the sapling of the first, growing into maturity and yielding fruit in twenty years, the shadow of which was for One Hundred and Eighty Years the delight of the land; and when its limbs had become time-worn, and when the species of the same fruit had become improved, other hands of men of like conscience inserted into its stock the scions of the latter, and in ten years growth we sit down under a foliage more thick and refreshing, and taste a fruit more highly flavored;—the whole bearing marks of longevity and freshness, never we trust to wither, or in its essential principle to change, while man needs a government. And truly the petition addressed at the Restoration of Charles II. sets forth, that "our fathers," who, in the beginning, "established a mutual liberty of conscience," which was "confirmed under their first Patent," "might be permitted to hold forth a lively experiment, that a most flourishing civil State may stand, and best be maintained, and that among English subjects, with a full liberty in religious concernments, aud that true piety rightfully grounded on gospel principles, will give the best and the greatest security to sovereignty, and will lay in the hearts of men the strongest obligations to true loyality." These two men fell on sleep, each in the place of his adoption; the eldest Mr. Williams, at Providence, in the Eighty fourth year of his age, having been born in 1599 and dying in 1683; and the younger, Mr. Clark, at Newport, in the Sixty seventh year of his age, having been born in 1609, and dying in 1676 Of the charters of these two men Callender said when nearly a century had passed, "The civil State has flourished, as well as if secured by ever so many penal laws, and an Inquisition to put them in execution. Our civil officers have been chosen out of every religious society, and the public peace has bcen as well preserved, and the public councils as well conducted, as we could have expected, had we been assisted by ever so many religious tests."

And unto this day in Rhode-Island we have nothing but common statute law to guard religious bodies; nor do we need any other than voluntary associations, secured as all other bodies politic are secured, by common and statute law. And I dwell upon historic fact to show that a state so free, has been as largely rewarded. No division of our confederacy has been, it is believed. more blessed than this State has been. Here there have prevailed some of the most glorious revivals; and the records of our older churches teem with illustrations of great grace. Our college too, founded on the same platform, has sent forth some of our ablest men. And although some in the possession of this great latitude have gone to extremes, yet we have nothing to do, but to repair to God directly for his blessing, and we become at the same time blessed, and are made blessings. It is in the absence of true spiritual reliance, and the consequent neglect of our obligations, that we have any occasion to write Ichabod upon any of our walls, for the glory of the Lord never departs from them who preserve his ark and keep his testimony.

The first Baptist Church in America was organized in Providence, as nearly as I can ascertain, in 1639. There can be no question that the founders of Providence, being mostly religious persons, held services on the Sabbath and at other times. But in the absence of all evidence that any Church of any religious persuasion was established by them until the one which was composed of individuals baptized by Roger Williams and others, I conclude that the Baptist Church formed in the same year of that event, was the first Church gathered in the Colony, and the first of its kind in the new settlements of America. The first fact is acknowledged in the records of the May Session of the Colonial Legislature in 1774, in which a petition presented from this Society for an Act of Incorporation is thus recorded:—" Whereas sundry persons belonging to the congregation assembling for the public worship of Almighty God, with the Christian Church, called Baptist or Antipœdobaptist, in the Town of Providence, *being the oldest Christian Church in this Colony*, and professing to believe that Water Baptism ought to be administered by immersion only, and that professed believers in Jesus Christ, and no others, are proper subjects to the same," &c. If this record be correct, it goes also to show that there was no Christian Church of any denomination in the Colony prior to 1639. By many it has been believed that Mr. Williams was chosen the " first pastor of the Church " which was established in that year, but to my mind there is no satisfactory evidence that he was ever inducted into its pastorate; or that he ever relinquished his views of the true mode of baptism, as has likewise been claimed, but simply of the authority of any person then living to perform it. In this opinion I am sustained by Mr. Callender, who has expressed his conviction in the words that I quote from his printed discourse in which he alludes to this point. He says, " It does not appear to me, that he had any doubt of the true mode, and proper subjects of baptism, but that no man had any authority to revive the practice of the sacred ordinances, without a new and immediate commission." And " had Mr.

Williams adhered to this maxim," (that the Bible contains the religion of Christians, and that the word of God is a sufficient rule of faith and worship,) the maxim of Protestants, and more especially of Puritans, he might have continued an Anabaptist all his days, as it is said he was more inclinable to them in his latter time."

In 1652–3, thirteen years after the formation of the Church, a division of sentiment concerning the laying on of hands upon the heads of new members as a divine ordinance took place among them, and subsequently they walked in two bodies, yet the members of both adhered to the same love of freedom in the exercise of conscience as existed in their beginning.

In a report like this it is desirable that we settle if possible the question, concerning the origin of the denomination in this country. As no Baptist Church existed in America beyond our Colonial limits before 1639, the field of our enquiry is directly before us. The existence of a Baptist Church in Providence as early as 1639, has been questioned by no one. But whether this Church is the first of the denomination in this country, has been disputed. Those who deny this fact rest their argument mainly on the following suppositions, viz: that the present Baptist Church in Providence is not the direct descent of the original membership, but of the dissenting portion; and that in 1638 there was a Baptist Church existing in another section of the Colony. In event of the truth of these two positions, the Church to which it has been from the beginning with little variation ascribed, turns out not to be the first in existence in our persuasion in this country. From all the facts, however, that I have been able to collect, I am satisfied that the received opinion concerning the first organization is correct and that on the second question there is room for inquiry.

The division itself in the Church in Providence in 1652–3, shows that a Baptist Church had existed previously to that date, and that in each division there were some of the first baptized; thus identifying the place where the new testament bäptisms in America were first performed. Concerning this fact there was no question among ancient historians as far as I can learn from their publications; a fact that chiefly interests me in this document. But of the organization of a Baptist Church in the town of Providence in 1639 there can be no question, and that some of the members of each division in 1652, had been members of that Church is, I think equally correct. T. Olney, Chad. Brown, (ancestor of the existing Brown family in Providence,) W. Wickenden, G. Dexter, all elders in the Church, were members of that fellowship. It has been said that this Church, because Mr. Williams did not remain with it, soon "crumbled to pieces," but Mr. Calender declares, "I believe this to be a mistake in fact, for it certainly appears, there was a flourishing Church of the Baptists there, a few years after the time of the supposed breaking to pieces; and it is known by the names of the members, as well as by tradition," (and this Mr. C. records of a period before the division of 1652–3) "they were some of the first settlers at Providence." And their successors remain till this day the faithful representatives of those noble sires who gave us, in the language of Roger Williams in 1644, this illustrious sentiment, that "every man has the absolute right to a full liberty in religious concernments." I say representatives, for it is evident that the main strength of the Church belonged to that portion of it which at the division continued, as the Church had always done, in the centre of the town, and from which all that has ever been of any special note to Baptists in Providence, or to the denomination at large, has emanated. As to the simple change in organization it is of small importance in itself, for there was no change in any doctrinal truth, nor in any religious practice, save in the practice of the imposition of hands upon the reception of members. So far as I can learn, there has never been, since 1639, a day when the members of the First Baptist Church in Providence were not the main medium for the transmission of Baptist principles, until 1805, the date of the present Pine street Baptist Church. It was not, as in the Congregational churches, in which divisions have occurred in doctrines involving the salvation of the soul; the change was concerning merely an external rite. And besides, in no part of Mr. Clark's writings, as I understand, did he allude to the baptism at Providence, in 1639, which, as it appears to me, he would naturally have done, if he were at that time a pastor of a Baptist Church in the Colony; and especially when Baptists needed so much the public sympathy. It is more probable that Mr. Clark himself formed his church after the model of the church then at Providence, as this church has always been what that church is said to have been, a "Five and not a Six Principle Baptist Church."

But as I am discussing the origin of the denomination in this country, I will not withhold in this place a brief analysis of the Historical Discourse, delivered by the Rev. John Callender, in the Sabbatarian meeting-house, in Newport, March 24th, 1738, (the late meeting-house of this church then being in process of erection) it being that day one hundred years since the Indian Sachems signed the deed of the Island. That discourse, to which

I often refer in this report, is a document of the highest authority, and as it comes from one of the honored pastors of the First Baptist Church in Newport, I use it with greater confidence.

In his exordium, Mr. Callender states his plan, arranged in three parts; viz: An account of the occasion and manner of the first settlement of the Colony; a view of its civil and religious history; and its present condition. Under the first he relates many things incident to the settlement of New England in general and of this Colony in particular;—such as the early history of Mr. Roger Williams—his flight from Massachusetts and his reception by the Indians in the land which he called Providence—also Mr. Williams' reception of John Clark and his associates, the purchase of Aquetneck, now called Rhode-Island, and the settlement of this Island. Under the second, Mr. Callender gives a very careful and minute account of the purchases made from the Indians of other lands also, that were in his times component parts of the Colony; the incorporations of the various towns, and their subsequent formation into counties; and the different forms of government that had prevailed in the territory. He proceeds then to give the information he he had obtained of the religious history of the Colony. And when he has completed this, he describes the condition of the Indians within the bounds of the Colony, and the circumstances of the English in regard to them. He closes his discourse with several admirably practical addresses.

It is his religious account that specially induces me to introduce this analysis. And I have described the main features of his plan that you may mark with what great care and accuracy he has compiled the facts which he has given. Having defended the views of religious liberty which had obtained in the Colony, accounting it as the greatest glory of the Colony to have avowed such sentiments as had been expressed from its settlement, while blindness yet existed in other places, he presents it as an example to others, because therein the principles were first put into practice. He then proceeds to relate in detail the religious history of the Colony. And you will notice the peculiar phraseology employed when he enters upon his civil history of the country. "And that we may take things from the beginning, be pleased," he says, "to observe that October 12, 1492, this part of the world since called America," &c. And in a note at this date he adds, "I have followed the dates in the New-England Cronology, where the most material facts are collected, and placed in the truest light, and the dates fixed with the greatest accuracy and exactness." And the same care is apparent in all his civil narrations. Nor has any discrepancy been detected save in his date of Williams' landing at Providence, which he fixes in 1634–5, one year earlier than the period now confirmed; but be it remembered that there has been a disagreement among historians of high repute concerning this point; but in all others he is wonderfully correct and even in this also according to Hopkins and Hutchinson. And the same care is apparent in his religious narative. In a manner similar to his civil, he commences his religious narrative, and almost in the same language. "But to take things in their order," (their order of occurrence certainly, in accordance with historical principles) "Mr. R. Williams is said, in a few years after his settling at Providence, to have embraced the opinions of the people called (by way of reproach) Anabaptists, in respect to the subject and mode of baptism; and to have formed a church there," which last named fact Mr. Callender in a note afterwards retracts. And subsequently, having made many remarks defending the importance of adhering to the plainly revealed institutions of Jesus Christ, notwithstanding the corruptions put upon them by men, (referring to Mr. Williams turning a seeker for a new revelation, by which men should be commissioned afresh to perform them,) Mr. Callender describes the division that took place in 1652 concerning the laying on of hands, in the church formed at the baptism of Williams, and the several branches that shot out from that church; and when Providence was divided in 1730 into several townships, he describes how these branches became distinct churches; and he informs us that there was in his day "a strict Association of all the Baptist Churches in N. England, that hold the same doctrine;" which Association continues to this time, having held its one hundred and eighty-third anniversary at Cranston, Sept. 9th, 10th and 11th, 1853, it having been formed in 1670. Mr. Callender next in order returns to Rhode Island, and gives us in detail certain facts concerning the first settlers. He styles them "Puritans of the highest form." He states that they depended on the assistance of Mr. Wheelright, a famous Congregational minister; and when disappointed by his non arrival, that Mr. Clark carried on a public worship, (as did Mr. Brewster at Plymouth,) at his first coming, till they procured Mr. Lenthel of Weymouth, who is specially spoken of as a teacher of youth in a public school. He states that they built a meeting-house both at Portsmouth and at Newport, but never intimates that they ever formed a church, as Gov. Winthrop has recorded, although he speaks of its having been "gathered in a very disorderly way." And from the remark added by Mr. Callender, I question whether there was any church on the Island, which was duly formed at that period, any more than at Providence in the beginning, for speaking of their Meeting house he writes, " which I suppose was *designed* for public worship," and which I doubt not was built for any other meetings of the colonists. And also from another passage near the close of the same discourse in which he mentions that his, (the Clark church,) " was the first society settled in church order on this Island, as it is the eldest ;" clearly implying, as it seems to me, that there was no regular church on the Island actually and properly constituted, until the one to which Mr. Callender ministered as the pastor in 1738, and which had then been in existence certainly from 1644, and probably from 1641.

Mr. Callender proceeds to give us what he has learned from others " that in 1644," as it was said, " Mr. Clark formed a church on the scheme and principles of the Baptists. It is certain," he adds, " that in 1648 there were fifteen members in full communion." He then describes successively in the order of their establishment the seven churches then existing on the Island, viz. The First Baptist in 1644; the Second Baptist in 1656; the Friends in 1656–7 ; the Sabbatarian in 1671 ; The First Congregational in 1696, the Church organized in 1720, and the one in 1728; the Episcopal in 1700, and the Friends at Portsmouth. And he closes his religious history with an equally particular mention of the several distinct Societies and worshipping Assemblies of Christians in the entire Colony, numbering thirty-three. If there be any excellence in this discourse, and there are very many, it is found in the correctness of the dates which he has affixed to the several events described; dates that so far as the Colonial records are involved I have found in every instance to be precisely as he has given them.

To my mind therefore it is conclusive that Mr. Callender himself has fully settled the question, and that he fully believed that the Baptist Church in Providence organized in 1639, was the first Baptist Church formed in America. He first describes the Church in Providence, not from courtesy as one might be tempted to do at this time, (for Newport was by far the more flourishing and prominent,) but as an historian; and then in the order of his history he comes to the church of his care, as being next in age. To doubt this is to invalidate his accuracy as an historian, and to excite doubts of the correctness of his order and dates in his civil history of New England in general and of this Colony in particular. And I have given the facts as I have found them narrated, believing most fully that they are faithfully chronicled from the highest and most reliable authorities; and that without any other motive than to adhere to what historical testimony establishes, so that we may possess the historical facts in our Ecclesiastical, as well as in our Civil History. And if any evidence exists to change the order of these events, no one will be more gratified than myself to receive it.

At the session of the Legislature in May, 1682, an act was passed confirming to Newport, Portsmouth, Providence, Warwick and Westerly the lands that had been purchased by these several towns of the Indians. At the session in 1703, the Colony was divided into two counties, Providence Plantations and Rhode-Island; and in June, 1729, it was again divided into three counties, in order that the interests of the citizens at large might be better subserved than they could be under the forms by which they had been heretofore conducted. The first embraced Newport, Portsmouth, Jamestown, and New Shoreham, and was known by the name of Newport County, Newport being its county town. It has been since that period increased by the addition of Middletown, Little Compton and Tiverton; it now includes seven towns. The second was styled the County of Providence, having Providence for its county town, and included Providence, East Greenwich and Warwick.—The towns within the present boundaries of the county have since been added, comprising ten; viz. Smithfield, Glocester, Scituate, Cumberland, Cranston, Johnston, North Providence, Foster, Burrillville and the City of Providence. The third county was denominated Kings County, and was composed of the towns of North Kingstown, South Kingstown, and Westerly, South Kingstown being the county town. The towns of Charlestown, Exeter, Richmond and Hopkinton have been annexed, and the name of the county altered to that of Washington; it numbers at this time seven towns. The County of Bristol was formed in the month of February, 1746, and consisted of the towns of Bristol and Warren, Bristol being the county seat. The town of Barrington has since been established, and added to this connty, so that it embraces three towns. In June, 1750, East Greenwich, that had been divided into East and West Greenwich, and Warwick, which had been also formed into two towns, the latter bearing the name of Coventry, were taken from Providence County, and made into a distinct County, which was called the County of Kent, and embraced four towns, East Greenwich being the county town. Thus the State has been apportioned into five counties, which divisions remain and afford to its inhabitants every accommodation that their civil interests apparently require, embracing in all thirty-one townships. I shall arrange my remarks upon the churches now existing in the State according to these divisions, beginning with the County of Newport.

County of Newport, established in 1729.

Tiverton, incorporated into a township in January, 1746, is one of the five towns that were annexed to the Rhode Island jurisdiction by the royal decision of George II. These towns were Tiverton, Little Compton, Bristol, Warren, and Cumberland. Their first meeting for the choice of town officers occurred on the second Tuesday in February, having been received into the State compact in January, and added to the counties to which they are attached, the last of February, 1746. Tiverton is the northern town of the County. It has a population of 5,000, with a property estimated at more than $2,000,000. There is a Roman Catholic house, seating 600 persons, and valued at $4,500, and another now in process of erection, at a cost, it is said, of more than $50,000 ; a Friend's, seating 200, and valued at $1,000 ; two Congregational, accommodating 600, with estates of $10,000 ; one Christian, seating 100, and valued at $1,500, which is now closed; one Free Will Baptist, arranged for 250, at a cost of $3,500; and one Associated Baptist.

The Central Baptist Meeting house was built in 1851, on the high lands, half of a mile north of the stone bridge. It is 36 ft.×48 ft., having a tower, orchestra, vestry, and convenient shed-room, and seats for 300, having a congregation of 200, averaging 90, 42 pews on the floor, and appraised at $2,500. The population in the vicinity is 466. They tax their pews and have also subscriptions for their minister's support. Their deacon is Asa Gray. Their late pastor, Rev. D. M. Burdick, has removed to Smithfield. It was by his means to a great extent that this house was erected. They have now no pastor. Here is an interesting field, and a residence peculiarly healthy, with a water view and landscape scenery rarely, if ever equalled. The house is placed in the centre of a county about nine miles square, in which it is the only edifice of the kind, except that of a small society of Friends. Only about $90, of its cost remains unpaid.

Little Compton, formed also into a township with corporate powers in January 1746, is the south-eastern town of the State, and is connected with Tiverton on the south. Its population is 1.600, and its property $1,000,000. There is an efficient Congregational church here, their house seating 500, and valued at $4,000 ; a Methodist also, holding 300, and valued at $4,000 ; a Friend's, providing for 200, at a cost of $1,000 ; and a Christian, having room for 300, and appraised at $2,500.

Portsmouth, originally called Pocasset, but denominated Portsmouth in 1644, is the north town on the Island of Rhode Island ; it was settled in March, 1637–8, the deed of the Indian Sachems Canonicus and Myantonomy, being dated the 24th of that month. It contains 2000 population, and its property is estimated at $1,500,000. There is a Methodist house here, having room for 300, and valued at $2,000 ; a Christian, seating 250, with a valuation of $1,000 ; a Friend's, accommodating 500, appraised at $2,500 ; and two Episcopalian houses providing for 600, and valued at $15,000.

4

MIDDLETOWN, set off from Newport in August, 1743, lies between Portsmouth and Newport, having a population of 1,000, with estates valued at $1,200,000. There are two Christian houses, seating each 200, the one valued at $500, and the other at $1,700 ; and an Episcopalian, designed to seat 150, which cost $1,500.

JAMESTOWN, which was purchased in 1657, and incorporated in May, 1678, embraces the Island of Canonicut; it numbers 400 inhabitants, and its property is valued at $300,000. This is a beautiful Island in the Narragansett bay, dividing the waters into the eastern and western channels, and is nine miles long by one broad, having an Episcopal house, seating 160, with a property of $600 ; a Friend's, accommodating 120, with an estate at $400 ; and a Free Will Baptist, with seats for 120, and a property of $350.

The four preceding towns have no house for the Associated Baptists, although among those on Rhode Island there are many families who worship with the Baptist churches in Newport, several members of which families being connected with these churches in gospel fellowship.

NEW-SHOREHAM, anciently called by the Indian name MANISSES, and afterwards Block-Island, as it is said, after one Adrian Block, a Dutch navigator, who came to this place, was made a township in May, 1672. It is situated thirty miles south-west from Newport, and fifteen from Point Judith, measuring eight miles in length and upon an average two and a half in breadth. It is a luxuriant Island, having 1,300 inhaitants, with a property estimated at $500,000. There are two Free Will Baptist Societies, one of which is now building a Meeting-house to seat 200, at a cost of $500; the other has no house. The house of the Associated Baptists is a one story building,

18 by 45 feet, containing 70 pews, seating 240, and valued at $400;—erected I should think in another age;—a house wholly unworthy of the Island. They need a new edifice exceedingly, and such a building would do more to promote the improvement of the people than any other external instrumentality. Their congregation is 300, averaging 150. The minister is sustained by subscription. The deacons are Edward Dodge and Simon Dodge.

Upon this Island there is scarcely a tree growing. The land presents an ocean surface, rolling every where in the form of waves moderately raised. There are only three places that can be said to be elevated, viz: Beacon-Hill, Pilot-Hill, and Clay-head-heights; these not only afford a fine prospect of the face of the Island, but they present on every side a magnificent view of the waters of the Atlantic. Clay-head on the north-east and the high bluffs on the southern boundary, each being some one hundred feet above the level of the ocean, give to those who are in the distance a favorable impression of the value of the Island; and could an adequate breakwater be constructed at the landing on the east-shore, it would become an invaluable harbor to many vessels, and bring into market at once all its land for summer residences, giving to its present owners a greatly increased price for their acres. A town appropriation of some $10,000 would build such a landguard and make it the resort of numbers. There is also a pond in the north-west part of the Island, containing it is said, nearly two thousand acres of surface, with a depth of from forty to sixty feet, which has been used as an harbor. The entrance to this pond was cut by an order from the Assembly in May 1670, but in process of time, it has been mostly filled up with the washing of the shore. Could this breach again be opened, this pond would afford one of the largest and safest harbors upon the entire coast. And I am happy to learn that both these suggestions are receiving consideration; and they will it is believed, ere long, lead to the elevation of this Island of the ocean.

It is in view of the future as well as the present inhabitants, that I regard this Island as being to us a very interesting place of labor. Isolated from society in general, the people, of necessity, have little more to interest them than what they themselves originate. Hence it is that there has been so much zeal among them at different periods, especially in religious things, and not according to knowledge. But they are thoroughly Baptist in their convictions and sympathies. And if the right means be employed, there is no reason why the investment should not prove a valuable one.

The morals of the inhabitants compare favorably with those of other communities. In a town meeting, about ten years since, they refused by a decided vote, to sanction the vending of intoxicating drinks, and hence none are retailed upon the Island. Education is receiving increased attention. There are five public schools, sustained in as many districts, each district meeting the expenses of its own school by taxation.

Newport was settled by John Clark, and others, who came from the northern to the southern part of the Island in the Spring of 1639. The settlers at Portsmouth had become too numerous for their personal advantage, and therefore they formed another settlement which constituted the southern division of the Island that gave the State its name. It contains 11.000 inhabitants, and by estimation $8.000.000 in property. In the year 1785 Newport became a city, but returned to its original town government after one year. In 1853 it again became a city; and the Hon. George H. Calvert presides with great efficiency as its first Mayor. The Redwood Library, 7000 volumes, under the management of its librarian Augustus Bush Esq., is of great public utility.

This city has become, during the warm weather, the most inviting place of resort on the sea-board, and already many costly and very splendid private residences have been erected in its late agricultural district, and on the cliffs that girt it on the ocean side. Various houses of this description have also been built in other parts of the city territory. The relative importance of this location is becoming appreciated as in the times of our fathers, when the business of the town was as active and extensive as that of any other place with like capital. In 1738 there were owned by the citizens, to say nothing of the large number of distilleries, rope-walks, and other branches of manufacturing interests, more than one hundred sail of vessels, and in 1769, the town "outrivalled New York, in her foreign and domestic commerce. The inhabitants of New York, New Haven, New London, &c. depended entirely on Newport for a market to supply themselves with foreign goods, and here they found a ready market for the produce of their own states. Eighteen West Indiamen have been known to arrive in a single day. It was said at that period, that possibly New York might, in time, equal Newport." And the direction of letters from Europe to persons in the present grand emporium of trade, was usually "New York, near Newport, R. I."

In this city there are fifteen congregations who meet regularly and five that assemble only occasionally.—Among these there are three Episcopal houses, seating 2.066 persons, with property attached valued at $41.000; one Free Will Baptist, now let to the Episcopalians ; one Seventh-day Baptist, accommodating 300, valued at $1000, in which also the Fourth or Free Will Baptist have an interest ; one Congregational, providing for 800, and estimated at $13.500 ; one Unitarian holding 700, and valued at $8.500 ; one Methodist Episcopal, seating 800, and appraised at $8.000 ; two Friends, accommodating 1800, with $21.000 in estate ; one Jewish Synagogue, now closed, seating 300, and estimated at $8.000; one Roman Catholic, holding 900, valued at $30.000, and one other not occupied ; one Union and two other colored churches, have room for 300, and are apprised at $2.000 ; a few smaller houses, and a Moravian now used as a school house; and three of the Associated Baptists. We may also add that a house for a Catholic School is being erected to be opened the ensuing Spring with accommodations for 100 girls ; it is to be under the care of the Sisters of Mercy. A school-house for boys is nearly completed, with accommodations for an equal number.

The First Baptist house was erected in 1846, and is capable of seating 950. It is situated on Spring street, measuring 62 by 72 feet, and is furnished with tower and bell, galleries and organ, having 120 pews on the floor, and vestries, at a cost of $10.000, It is a substantial and commodious building, and has no debt. The congregation is 700, averaging 450. They support their pastor by a society taxation. The deacons are Benjamin

Smith, Peleg Sanford, Benjamin B. Howland, and Samuel S. Peckham.

The first pastor of this church was JOHN CLARK, who came from England to this country, in 1637, and who was the founder of the Colony which first settled upon the soil of the Island. The Baptists of this Island justly claim this church as their mother and Mr. Clark as their ancestor. In the very beginning of the civil government, a congregation was gathered, not however with much form or efficiency, composed of persons bound together principally by the one and the grand idea of their times, liberty of conscience in religious sentiment, and its peaceable enjoyment, independent of the civil power. This people "had desired and depended on the assistance of Mr. Wheelwright, a famous Congregational minister," a man of kindred feelings with theirs, but who for some unassigned reason did not take up his abode with them, but went to Long Island. Subsequently, after about two years ministry performed among them by Mr. Robert Lenthall of Weymouth, a teacher of a school as well as a minister of the gospel, Mr. Clark resumed the care of the public meetings, as he had done prior to the settlement of Mr. Lenthall; and as Gov. Winthrop records that in 1641 there was "a schism among them," on account of the erronious opinions of one Nicholas Easten and others, it has been inferred that they became extinct and that the distinct and separate organization of the present church then took place. Under date of Oct. 12th, 1648, there are recorded the names of twelve persons as members, the pastor Mr. Clark and his wife, and ten others; the first baptisms recorded are of Samuel Hubbard and two others, which occured the month ensuing, Nov. 3d, thus confirming the statements made by

Callender, " It is said that in 1644 Mr. John Clark and some others formed a Church on the scheme and principles of the Baptists. It is certain that in 1648 there were fifteen members in full communion." The impression of several historians is that it was formed earlier than in 1644. But it is evident that no other than Mr. Clark exercised any efficient pastoral supervision on the Island from its settlement in 1638, until his return to England with Mr. Williams in 1651.

This is a venerable church, having existed for more than two centuries. Located in a place so well known and so popular as Newport was for many years, which excelled Providence in capital and in the number of its inhabitants until the revolutionary war, (that war so destructive in every respect to Newport,) this church occupied a high rank in the community, and drew members from towns remote. It has enjoyed the ministry of many who were distinguished for the purity of their life and for their clear conceptions of the gospel. And never in the severest temptation has it as a body relinquished the truth as it is in Jesus. And at no former period has it been more prosperous than it is at the present time.

The Second Baptist house was erected in 1834–5, and dedicated October 22d, 1835. It is situated on the corner of North Baptist and Farewell streets, and is of Gothic architecture, 86 by 52 feet, having 104 pews on the floor, and seating 1000; its property is rendered at $25,000. The congregation is 600, averaging 350. It is furnished with a tower and bell, galleries, organ and vestries. It also has a parsonage house. The pastor is supported by the income of a fund and by subscriptions. The deacons are Sanford Bell, Benjamin Marsh, John C. Barker, and Simeon Hazard. This church, like the first, has been favored with many revivals of religion and has always adhered to the faith. It is also venerable in age, having been constituted in 1656, nearly two hundred years ago.

The Central Church, which emanated from the Second in 1846, has a congregation of 700, with an average of 450. At their organization Jan. 7th, 1847, they purchased the Second Congregational Meeting house, standing in a central location on Clarke Street, (a finely framed building, built in 1735,) and entirely remodeled it the same year, dedicating it anew the 23d of September following. It is finished with a tower, galleries, and vestries, has a bell and organ, and will seat 900. It has on the floor 104 pews, and measures, since its enlargement in 1852, 93 by 42 feet; it has cost the Society $12.000. Unwilling to sell their pews, the Society owes a debt of $6.237, the premises being a stock debt in shares of 100 each, at semi-annual interest, conditional in its redemption, secured by a peculiar form of mortgage on the premises, and a policy of insurance of $7.000. It has paid one half of its outlay. It rents its pews, the proceeds of which, with weekly contributions, fully and punctually meet their expenses. Every male member of the Church of twenty-one years of age, in good standing in the Church, is a member of the Society. Its deacons are Joseph W. Hazard, Gideon Lawton, Nathaniel H. Langley, and Thomas Mumford Seabury. This is an enterprising and thriving body, strongly attached one to another, and deeply interested in the principles of their organization.

The actual property in the county of Newport amounts to $14.500.000, and the population is 22.300. In the houses of public worship, there are 17.206 seats, valued at $240.950.

In this County the Associated Baptists have not quite one-fifth of the accommodation in the churches, but in the city they have more than one-fourth. "The people who came to Rhode-Island were," as Callender maintains, "Puritans of the highest form." And quoting from Bishop Sanderson he further states what the Bishop declared, that "the Rev. Archbishop Whitgift, and the learned Hooker, men of great judgment, and famous in their times, did long since foresee and declare their fear, that if ever Puritanism should prevail among us, it would soon draw in Anabaptism after it.—This Cartwright and the Disciplinarians denied, and were offended at.—But these good men judged right; they considered, only as prudent men, that Anabaptism had its rise from the same principles the Puritans held, and its growth from the same course they took; together with the natural tendency of their principles and practices towards it; especially that ONE PRINCIPLE, as it was then by them misunderstood, that the Scripture was the adequate rule of action, so as nothing might be lawfully done, without express warrant, either from some command or example therein contained; which clue, if followed as far as it would go, would certainly in time carry them as far as the Anabaptists had then gone." "This" says Mr. Callender, "I beg leave to look upon as a most glorious concession of the most able adversaries." The first comers to this Island being absorbed in the great Principle of their day, (for an adherence to which many of them had been excommunicated from their churches in Massachusetts,) were led in their religious course to a result perfectly natural, the gradual and in the end full reception of Baptist sentiments. And hence it is that there is not for more than sixty years after their settlement, a record or a tradition of a pedo-baptism, nor any evidence that any other baptism than that of the New Testament was administered until after the close of the seventeenth century, when Congregationalists and Episcopalians began to come in.

And most sincerely do we hope for the continuance and increase of a representation of these early and truth-seeking settlers in a section so rich in natural scenery, and so justly celebrated for its salubrious climate; where too so much interest is felt in education and in morals, although much abounding fashionable dissipation is tolerated by many. We need in this garden of nature, faithful representatives who will successfully urge the claims of the gospel. But it is a matter of devout gratitude to Almighty God, that so much of the ministry as is now performed within this County is marked with such discriminating truth, although they sympathise not with us in the divine ordinance of baptism, and do not use its abundant waters for the emblematical burial of converts with Christ, "born not of blood, nor of the will of the flesh, nor of the will of man, but of God."

Leaving New Shoreham the 28th of July, the next day I visited Wickford, and thus entered what was denominated in June 1729, Kings County, but which in October 1781 was changed by an Act of the Legislature to its present designation,

Washington County, Incorporated in 1779 and 1781.

As the occasion and the reasons for this Act were peculiar and also the year itself memorable in the annals of our American history, I transcribe the entire record as found in the Schedule for that period. The

General Assembly were then in session at Kingston, the County town; the act stands unaccompanied by any explanation, and reads as follows, viz:

"Whereas since the Declaration of the Independence of the United States of America, it becomes the wisdom of the rising Republic to obliterate, as far as may be, every Trace and Idea of that Government which threatened our destruction—

"Be it enacted by the General Assembly, and by the Authority thereof it is hereby enacted,

That the Name of King's County, by which the Southernmost County in this State was heretofore distinguished, shall forever hereafter cease: And that, in perpetual and grateful Remembrance of the eminent and most distinguished Services, and heroic Actions, of the illustrious Commander in Chief of the Forces of the United States of America, the said County shall forever hereafter be known and called, in all legislative Acts, legal Proceedings, Convenances, &c. by the Name and Style of WASHINGTON."

And the citizens of the Kingstons, having had the name of Washington conferred upon the County, have felt, as I infer from their silence on this subject, that no harm can befall them, if the Colonial designations of their towns remain.

This County originally, when a Colony, embraced two of the Providence plantations; the first included the Kingstons, and the second the District of Westerly. Kingston, or the lands properly called the Narragansett lands, was incorporated into a township in October, 1674, but was subsequently in May, 1722, divided into North and South Kingston. And in March, 1742, North

Kingston was divided, by the constitution of another township, which was named Exeter.

NORTH KINGSTON contains three churches of the Associated Baptists, each possessing a neat and convenient edifice, centrally situated, and surrounded by a population greater in number than they can respectively accommodate with seats.

The First Church located their house on the Post-road, so called, a road that runs from Providence direct to the south-west corner of the State, in the village of Allenton, two miles south of Wickford; it was built in 1848, at a cost of $2000 ; it measures 32 by 47 feet. It contains 54 pews and an orchestra, reported as seating 400, with a congregation of 300, averaging 150. Rev. J. A. Tillinghast, their former minister, has returned to his charge after a year's absence. He is supported by subscription. The deacons are Constant Sweet and George Allen.

The second, which emanated from the preceding church, bears the name of the "First Baptist Church in Wickford," an incorporated village. Their house was erected in the centre of the place, (40 by 50 feet,) in 1816, and rebuilt in 1836. It is furnished with tower, bell, orchestra, and organ, and has on the floor 64 pews, seating 450. Their congregation is 300, averaging 160. The property is put down at $4000. A building near the church two stories high, has recently been erected at a cost of $700. The upper part is neatly seated for a chapel, holding 225, and the lower part is occupied for school purposes. They support their pastor by subscription. Temperance and morals in other respects prevail in the village, and an increasing attention is paid to education. They have at present no deacons, but older members serve at the table.

The third was built in 1842, about three miles north of Wickford, on the Post-road in that part of the town called "Quoitnesset." It is 36 by 46 feet, has an orchestra, tower, and 50 pews, holding 300; it has a congregation of 200, averaging 125. There is a population in their vicinity of about 550, who are temperate, and, as I am informed, otherwise well disposed. The edifice was finished at a cost of $2,000. Donations are made to the pastor for his services. The deacons are Charles Spencer and Thomas Hill.

In addition to these, there are in the town two Episcopal Churches, (one unoccupied,) seating 600 and valued at $7,600; one Methodist seating 150 and appraised at $300; one Free Will Baptist holding 150 and valued at $1,000; and two old or Six Principle Baptists accommodating 425 and valued at $1,800. The town contains 3,100 inhabitants and an aggregate property of $1,500,000.

Exeter, a division of North Kingston, was incorporated in March, 1742, into a township and called by this name. It is the northwestern town of the county. It has a population of 1,700 inhabitants and property estimated at $600,000. In the United States census of 1850, by which I am mainly governed in my statistics in every place, except such as relate to the immediate membership and Sabbath School department of our own churches, I find but two religious societies reported, and these in the eastern section, leaving the entire western without any stated place for worship. The first is the old Baptist, seating 400, and valued at $1,500; and the second, the Associated Baptist house, built in 1838; it is 32 by 42 feet, and free from debt. It is finished with tower, orchestra and 54 pews. It holds 400, has a congregation of 250, averaging 100, and is valued at $2,500. The minister is sustained by subscription. The singing is congregational. Temperance is promoted, and schools for the greater portion of the year are taught. They have no deacons.

South Kingston is contiguous to North Kingston, containing 4,000 people, with an estimated property of $1,600,000. There are two Episcopal houses, seating 580, valued at $4,500 ; two of the Friends providing for 650, at a cost of $1,600 ; two for colored people and others, containing 250 seats, at a cost of $800 ; one Congregationalist accommodating 500, with a property of $7,700 ; two of the Free Will Baptists holding 450, and appraised at $1,500 ; one of the Six Principle Baptist seating 150 and valued at $200 ; one of the Seventh-Day Baptists designed for 150 and valued at $700 ; and three of the Associated Baptists. There is also a house at the South Ferry, beautiful in its construction, the land on which it stands having been given to the Associated Baptists by John and Jacob Wanton.

The First Baptist Church has a house situated in the village of Wakefield, on the Post-road, having Peacedale on the north. It was built in 1852, is 37 by 70 feet, and cost $8,000. It is Gothic in its architecture both internal and external, and the whole style is peculiarly neat in all its finish. It has a tower, bell, orchestra, vestries, a fine lot, and a beautiful baptizing place opposite ; the whole exhibiting an enterprise worthy of the means of the society. It is decidedly the best house which I visited in the south part of the State. There are 92 pews, seating 600, which is the number of the congregation, averaging 400. The minister is sustained by pew rents. They have a population of 2,000. The deacons are N. C. Peckham and N. C. Armstrong.

The Second is built on the same road six miles south-west, in Perryville, the ancestry place of the Erie Perry. It was erected in 1845 and is 28 by 38 feet, has an orchestra and 26 pews, seating 300, congregation 150, averaging 100, and is valued at $1,500. There is a population of 310 in their vicinity. Their minister is sustained by subscription. The deacons are Joseph W. Brown and Edward H. Peckham. This church promises well, and needs encouragement. They have a property, as per tax list, of $34,000 only.

The Third is located in the north-west corner of the town, in the village of Usquepaug, on Queen's River, was built in 1849, having a tower, and orchestra, and is in dimensions 32 by 40 feet; it has 34 pews on the floor seating 300. It cost $1.200. This church should lay themselves out for Christ and souls. Their congregation numbers 125, and averages 60. The pews are rented, but the pastor sustains himself chiefly by his manual industry, which no church should allow. How much better could he have the privilege of studying that his profiting might appear unto all, and his congregation be trained to intelligence and an active piety. The building is estimated at $1.200, and is well situated. The deacons are J. T. Hopkins and Benjamin Lock.

Each of these edifices is free from debt, and appears to advantage to the traveller; but it is to be regretted that there is so little taste manifested in some other sections, where there is equal, and much greater means. The neat church in the New England village has been justly spoken of as its ornament; certainly it is its safety, if it be duly improved.

There is at Kingston Hill an interesting Academy, instituted by the Congregationalists, which is now under very favorable auspices. Rev. Joel Mann has been mainly instrumental in its organization and success. Such institutions, when like this, conducted in a catholic spirit are the safeguards of the age, and in no way so beneficially to the community can property be devoted, for if we can educate our youth properly, under God, we may expect the happiest results in society at large, as well as in domestic circles.

Westerly, embraces the land in the south western section of the State. It was purchased of the Indians, (by whom it was known by the name of Misquamicut,) in 1665, and was constituted a township in May, 1669, bearing the name of Westerly, from its geographical position. At the time of its purchase it comprehended all the land at present included within its present, and the boundaries of the respective towns of Charlestown, Richmond, and Hopkinton. Although its southern boundary is the Long Island Sound, the Pawcatuck river now forms its western and northern, and the town of Charlestown its eastern limit. Its population is 3500, and the estimation of its property is $1.500.000. The enterprise of its citizens and especially in the village at the Bridge where the citizens pass from their own into the territory of Connecticut, and their economy and general habits will ensure it a constantly increasing prosperity.

There are in this town two Sabbatarian Baptist houses seating 600, and valued at $6.200; one Christian Society's accommodating 300, and appraised at $3.500; one Episcopal providing for 300, with a property estimated at $5.000; one Methodist occupying the building known as the "Union," which seats 400, and is valued at $4.500; and three Associated Baptists.

At Lottery Village, five miles from Long Island Sound, there is a neat building belonging to the Baptist Church. It has a tower, orchestra, and 31 pews, and measures 26 by 36 feet. It was built in 1849 at a cost of $1.200, and is capable of seating 250 persons. The congregation is 150 averaging 25. Notwithstanding the Pawcatuck river runs on the western shore of the entire place and the water is very bold, the village is in the wane. At present the Bridge Village takes the business of the region, but there is every reason to anticipate that ere long active shipbuilding, or some manufacturing enterprise will be introduced, by which it will greatly increase. On this account it is an object to sustain the church, at least moderately, that it die not. There are now but 250 inhabitants belonging to the village, several of whom are absent at sea. Their deacon, Lyman Hall, in the absence of a pastor, labors to maintain preaching every other Sabbath; and on the alternate Sabbaths he holds a prayer meeting. As they report their property at $25.000, and as evidently prayer is wont to be offered there, we may hope they will yet live. The village, it is said, derived its name from the fact that the original owner of the land obtained a grant for a lottery; and having laid it out into house lots, put them up and drew them out in the form of prizes, the successful tickets entitling the holders to the lots represented by their numbers.

The Church at the Bridge is surrounded by a population of 2.000. It was erected in 1845, and with their parsonage is valued at $6.000. Its dimensions are 38 by 62 feet; it has a tower, bell, orchestra, vestries, and

66 pews seating 450. The congregation is reported 450, 300 being the average attendance. The pastor is sustained by subscription. The deacons are J. R. Vincent, T. H. Vincent, J. T. Thurston, and A. Buel. They have no debt. They are united and zealous, temperate, and promote useful education in all its forms. They have an interesting religious feeling prevailing among them, and are an able and very efficient church.

In the north-east corner of the town, at Doorville is another house, called the "Niantic," erected in 1851, 28 by 38 feet, and estimated at $1.000 ; it is finished with a tower, and has 38 slips seating 200. They have a debt of $110. The congregation is 100, and averages 60. The deacon is George W. Champlin. The population in its vicinity is about 500. The Society, although they possess not exceeding $12.000, are willing to pay liberally to sustain the gospel among them. There is now another factory in process of erection in this place, the owner of which said to his Superintendent, "I am not a resident, but never fail to put my name to any sum you put to your own." The village is increasing. The location of the church is in a neat lot; the whole impression upon my mind was favorable. The superintendent, who is altogether the wealthiest man in the church, named to me that a clergyman said to him while yet a boy, as he was passing down the Narragansett bay, "My boy, if you will, you can make a man." He said his heart at once responded, "Then a man will I be." And a man he has become indeed in the world, and also in Christ as I trust.

Charlestown, which lies east of Westerly, was taken therefrom in August, 1738, and constituted a township, and named Charlestown in honor of Charles II.

who granted the late State Charter; an instrument of almost two hundred years power, which was, and is, and ever will remain the true exponent of liberty, conscience, and right. If it had faults, it had virtues too; such as the world never saw before; virtues which governments must acknowledge and incorporate in their systems of government, or they cannot govern.

Charlestown is mainly an agricultural district, but its farms being principally owned abroad, will account for the fewness of its population. They are to a large extent tenants, and hence in all the town, large as it is, there are reported only 1.000 people, upon a property of $322.000. Within the boundaries of this town is the Indian settlement, the last of the powerful Narragansetts, real or mixed, numbering however at this time not more than one hundred souls. Their house of worship seats 150, and is valued at $200. There is also a Free will Baptist house seating 250, and valued at $1.500.

The Associated Baptist Meeting-house was built in 1840 on the post road eight miles south-west from the Second South Kingston church, and is in dimensions 34 by 40 feet; having an orchestra and 40 pews, the whole valued at $1.500. It is a neat building, having a large open lot, and is well situated. It will seat 300, and is not in debt. The congregation is 100, averaging 75. The deacon is Bowen Briggs. Some 350 people live in the region of the house; a region sadly injured by the use of spirituous liquors, as too many of our towns and cities bear fearful and appalling evidence; but nevertheless the people there should be encouraged; our efforts in this place we have reason to hope will not be in vain.

North and South Kingston and the two preceding towns lie upon the Narragansett Bay and Long Island Sound, and afford beautiful scenery. The large ponds of water flowing in from the ocean, that stretch along the southern boundary of Charlestown, are objects of great interest. And when the permanent inhabitants shall become the owners of the large and fertile farms that lie upon their shores, as I think they ultimately will, we may look for better religous influences in this section. The Convention has done a good and most valuable service for this entire line, and the pastor is prudently, but efficiently carrying out its instructions.

RICHMOND was a part of Charlestown until incorporated into a separate township in August, 1747 ; it contains a population of 1.800, with a property appraised at $600.000. There is a Seventh-day Baptist house seating 450, and valued at 1.600 and a Six Principle or General Baptist, accommodating 500, with a valuation of 1.500.

The Associated Baptist house, measuring 30 by 38 feet, is put down as seating 400, and at a value of $1000, much more than it is worth, unless this is the appraisal of its lot of ground. It was erected in 1785, and is tottering through the infirmities of age, not having been nursed in its strength. Either it was built in the woods, a mile and more from the present villages, or else the people have removed from it; certainly it should be taken down, having served its generations sufficiently, and a new one put up in the neighborhood of Kenyon's, Clark's, and Shannock's mills, three villages in near proximity with each other, having together at least 600 people within their influence, but where there is no house of public worship. The minister is sustained by subscription. He labors under every disadvantage, not however because, as I presume, the ancient edifice is in debt, for there is no such incumbrance. And yet this people report some $60.000 in the congregation, nearly one half of which is owned among the church members. The same report speaks well of the practical influence of temperance, and of the population generally;—and I saw no reason why they should not at once arise and build a house for Christ, in which the people who have no carriages to ride in, (which is true of the major part,) can assemble and be comfortable; for they do not now assemble in windy weather, because their house is open and cold, nor in the storm, for if they should, they could not keep it dry because of the rain that penetrates within. This field, I regard as one which ought to receive our immediate attention, and as one of great promise. The congregation is now only 80, averaging 50, when it might be hundreds. The deacon is J. Briggs.

Hopkinton, lying west from Richmond, and north of Westerly, a second division of Westerly, was incorporated in March, 1757. It contains 2.500 inhabitants, and not less than $700.000 in property. There are two societies of Friends, whose houses seat 300, and are valued at $1.500; three Seventh-day Baptist, seating 1.600, with a property of $10.500; one Methodist accommodating 200, and estimated at $1.200; and two Regular Baptist.

First. At Hopkinton city, the house is 30 by 40 feet, having a tower, orchestra, and 32 pews. It seats 150, and is estimated at $1.500; it has a congregation of 60, averaging 40; it was built in 1836. There is a population of 250, among whom the Seventh-day congregation numbers 125, and the two Friends, 50. The

Associated members are valued at $31.000, and the Society in addition $32.000. The deacons are Oliver D. Cole, and Robert Palmer. Many of the population in the interior attend service in the city village. The minister deceased during the past season. They support the house by subscription. They have no debt.

Second. The other church house, built in 1845, is situated in "Locust village," seven miles north, joining Brand's Iron Works, and is in a good location, having in the rear a beautiful baptizing pond. It is 34 by 45 feet, having tower, orchestra, vestries, sheds, bell, and 50 pews, (and no debt,) at a cost of $5.000. It seats 350 persons, and the congregation is 300, averaging 150. They rent their pews. The deacons are W. R. Greene and James C. Bakêr. It is an interesting church, exerting a wholesome influence. A revival of religion is enjoyed by them this autumn.

I have now compiled the facts touching the seven towns in Washington Couuty. It will be seen that the population numbers 17.600; that there are houses of worship to accommodate 14.355; that the property invested in church building is $105,500; and that the total valuation of the several towns amounts to $6.822.000. In very many neighborhoods there is little attention given to christian obligation, and fields are numerous for christian labor; a section of country affording abundant evidence to prove that such effort will fully reward the expenditure that ought there to be made.

Bristol County, formed in 1746.

Bristol was incorporated in January 1746 and in February became the county-town. It has a population of 5.000, and a capital of $3.400.000. It has six meeting-houses for public worship. The Episcopal seats 900, and is valued at $15.000; the Methodist accommodates 700, and is rated at $3.000; the Congregational provides for 800, and the church property is put down at $17.650; the Christian has room for 400, and property worth $3.500, and the Colored has 120 seats, and a valuation of $500.

The meeting-house of the First Baptist Church was built of stone, on High street, in 1814, and is in dimensions 45 by 65 feet, having a tower, bell, orchestra, organ and two vestries, 68 pews on the floor, and is free from debt. It is a substantial edifice, beautifully frescoed and cost $10.000. It will seat 500, their congregation being 400, averaging 150. The deacons are Reuben Oatley and George Fish. They have heretofore had numerous difficulties to encounter, but their prospects are now encouraging, and I trust they are destined to be favored abundantly of the Lord.

WARREN, incorporated in Jan. 1746, with its 3.300 inhabitants, has four edifices devoted to public worship. The Methodist have a flourishing church, their house seating 1.000, and valued at $14.000. The Episcopal is rated at 600 seats, and in property $13.000; and the Roman Catholic, opened since the census of 1850, is put down at 300 seats, and their house at $700.

The house of the regular Baptists is situated on the corner of Main and Miller streets, built of stone, 70 by 84 feet, with a tower 23 feet square, and is in style the Medium Gothic, having 146 pews on the floor, an orchestra, and seats 900; it is furnished with an organ, bell, and church furniture every way corresponding with such a noble structure. The building contains besides the audience room, a lecture, committee, study and other rooms of like appropriate character; it was erected in 1844 on a lot of land 145 feet square, tastefully arranged and beautifully decorated, at a cost of $18.000 ; it has no debt. The estimated value of property is $20.000. The congregation numbers 750, and the average attendance in ordinary weather, the standard adopted for every church, 500. The minister is sustained partly by a fund, but principally by voluntary subscription. The late pastor, Rev. Robert A. Fyfe, resigned in July, having performed an excellent ministry of the word among them. They are now destitute. The deacons are Stephen Mason, Stillman Welch, Lewis Howe, and Jacob Sanders. This is an able and efficient church and society, and an honor to religion and humanity.

It was in this town that the Rhode-Island College, founded in 1764, held its first commencement. The Warren Institute for young ladies, and the Warren Classical School for young men, are in the immediate neighborhood of this church, and share largely in the sympathies of this people. The estimate of property in the town is $2.000.000.

Barrington, which was separated from Warren on account of the difficulty of passing the Warren river, and incorporated into a distinct township in June 1770, has a population of 900, and a property of $600.000. It has only one religious interest, a Congregational church, whose meeting-house is valued at $7.000 ; it will accommodate 500 persons. This house has been recently repaired and ornamented with a tower and other improvements. The congregation, it is said, is prosperous.

The aggregate amount of real and personal estate in Bristol County is estimated at $6.000.000 ; its population at 9.200, and the number of seats in its houses of religious service 6.720, valued at $104.350. It is a section of country possessing much interest; its scenery is beautiful, and its commercial and manufacturing advantages are great. A rail-road is under contract, to run north and south from Providence, and to terminate in Bristol. The education of youth is diligently pursued, and temperance, and morals in general, are maintained. The inhabitants are in the main enterprising and industrious, and a good christian spirit prevails among the churches. We may hope to receive here a rich harvest for the glorious husbandman.

County of Kent, incorporated in 1750.

This section was a part of Providence County until June, 1750.

East Greenwich, its county town, was originally a tract of land in the Narragansett country south of Warwick, which upon the application of its inhabitants became a township in October 1677. It was extended to the western line of the Colony in October 1706, and divided in April 1741 into another township which was named West Greenwich. It has a population of 2.500, and is estimated in property at $800.000. There is an Episcopal Church seating 350, and valued at $5.000; a Friend's, holding 400, and appraised at $3.000; a Methodist accommodating 400, and valued at $5.000; and one Associated Baptist seating 470, congregation 250, average 150. The house, built in 1846 46 by 60 feet, has a debt of $700. It is finished with tower, orchestra, bell, organ, 80 pews, and is valued at $4.500. The deacon is James Tilley. The pews are rented. It is a good house, well located, and is an important station, having a large surplus of population who worship not in any regular place. They have recently settled a pastor. In the village there is a self-sustaining Literary Academy which promises great good to the community at large, under the direction of the Methodist Episcopal denomination.

There is also in the interior at French-town, so called, a building styled the "Seminary," estimated to seat 200, and in valuation $500. In this house and also in an old meeting-house at Noose Neck Hill, in West Greenwich, the Warwick and East Greenwich Baptist Church, numbering 80 members, hold service once a month. The deacons are W. Spencer, G. Bailey and D. H. Wightman.

West Greenwich, a portion of East Greenwich, incorporated as a township in April 1741, has 1.400 inhabitants and a property appraised at $453.000. There is at Noose Neck Hill a meeting-house occupied by the Associated Baptists as just stated, estimated to seat 600, and valued at $1.000. The congregation numbers 100, and averages 50. There is another occupied by the Old Baptists, seating 300, and valued at $500. The Rev. John Tillinghast holds religious services regularly at private houses, his church, the West Greenwich Baptist Church, having no house. There is an Old Baptist Church of 67 members, and a Free Will Baptist of 65 members, who also in these houses conduct public worship. The deacons of the Associated Baptist Church are Josiah Greene and Allen Tillinghast.

Warwick was purchased by Samuel Gorton and others, of the Indian Narragansett Sachem Myantonomy, Jan. 12th, 1342–3, and named in honor of the Earl of Warwick, who gave them his friendly protection.

It embraced originally what now forms the County of Kent. The present division, now properly the town of Warwick, contains 8.000 inhabitants and $3.500.000 of property. There are four Six-Principle Baptist houses, seating 1030, and appraised at $3.500 ; three Free Will Baptist accommodating 550, and valued at $3.200 ; one Congregational seating 250, and valued at $1.500 ; one Friends, holding 100, and put down at $250 ; one Sweedenborgian providing for 75 and at a cost of $400 ; one Roman Catholic accommodating 600, and valued at $1.000 ; two Episcopal holding 350, and appraised at $1.800 ; one Methodist seating 370, and valued at $2.000 ; one Union said to hold 400, and estimated at $2.500 ; and four Associated Baptists. The house of the Gortonites, if in being, is near Old Warwick Centre.

The First Baptist Church was built at Crompton Mills in 1843 ; its dimensions are 40 by 60 feet. It has a tower, orchestra, vestry, bell, and 64 pews, which they rent ; its property is estimated at $2.500 ; it has a debt of $300. It will hold 470, has a congregation of 175, the average attendance of which is 75. The church owns a parsonage valued at $800. The deacon is Pardon Spencer. These are good premises, but the foreign population has been so extensively introduced as to afford serious impediments to the efforts of the church. I trust they will labor to give to the new comers the Gospel also. Has not God sent them among us to receive good at our hands. Their souls are equally precious with ours, and without repentance toward God and faith in our Lord Jesus Christ,

> "No bleeding bird, nor bleeding beast,
> Nor hyssop branch, nor sprinkling priest,
> Nor running brook, nor flood, nor sea,
> Can wash the dismal stain away."

The Lippitt and Phenix meeting-house was built in Phenix village January 1842. It is 36 by 48 feet, with tower, bell, orchestra, organ, vestry, and 56 pews, which are rented, with the proceeds of which and subscriptions the minister is maintained. It cost $3.000. It has a debt of $1.800, provided for by stock at 5 per cent. A parsonage has been built the past year. The congregation is 300, averaging 165. The house seats 400. The deacons are J. B. Tanner and J. Bailey, There are 5.000 people in the community, a large proportion of whom are foreigners. The temperance pledge of entire abstenance from alcoholic liquors is a condition of membership, it being one of the articles of their covenant. This has been one of the most promising churches, but difficulties have long existed among them. There is now a better prospect. I have spent two Sabbaths, and in connection with Rev. Wm. Coggswell several other days, endeavoring to remove these difficulties, and I trust with divine favor. Most of those who had been heretofore active in the church, have returned to their communion. Situated in a pleasant country and surrounded with many things attractive, it is expected that the members of this church will continue to fulfil the high expectations that are indulged concerning them, and which have been heretofore so liberally redeemed. The Rev. Mr. Coggswell, who added greatly to their strength and usefulness by his counsels, has removed to Minesota; in his departure Rhode-Island loses a valuable minister who has not failed to do all he could to advance the interests of our Zion.

Near to this interest and on the same branch of the Pawtuxet river is the village of Natic. The meeting-house was erected by Gov. W. Sprague in 1839, and was long styled the "Union." It is now rented by him to the Natic Baptist Church. It is 40 by 54 feet, and has a tower, bell, orchestra, vestry, and 58 pews. Its value is $2,500. Some 1500 people live in the neighborhood. The house seats 400, congregation is 275, averaging 200. The pastor is sustained by pew rents and subscriptions. The deacons are Christopher Warren, Smith W. Pearce, and Henry A. Bowen. This church, it is believed, is one of much hope.

In near proximity to this community there is the Point village, and the new one now building by Gov. Sprague called Wakefield, which united with the Point, presents an inviting field of labor not yet improved by any denomination. A member living in Centerville, has in reserve a lot of land for a Baptist Church, well situated for such a building.

Some seven miles east is another of the Churches of the Associated Baptists, called the "Shawomut Baptist Church of Old Warwick." They worship in the house belonging to the Old Baptists, who very seldom occupy it. It was erected in 1829. It measures 34 by 42 feet, and is valued at $800. It will seat 300, has a congregation of 100, averaging 80. The pastor is sustained by subscription. The deacon is B. Green. The church owns a neat parsonage upon which there is a debt of $400. It cost $1,500. There is no other meeting in this part of the town, and hence it is a lighthouse the lamp of which should be kept filled, trimmed and burning.

Coventry, incorporated in August 1741, was set off from Warwick. It contains 3,800 inhabitants and a valuation in property of $1,800,000. There are three Six Principle Baptist's houses seating 600, and valued at $2,250; one Congregational accommodating 300 and estimated at $1,500; and two Associated Baptists.

The Central Baptist Meeting-house, built in Washington village in 1839, measures 36 by 50 feet, will seat 400, and is valued at $1,500. The congregation is 400, averaging 200. It has 50 pews. Also a debt of $330. It has an orchestra. The population in the vicinity is 1000. For years this church and its minister, Rev. Albert Sheldon, have been connected with the General Baptists, but during the last year they have united with the Associated Baptists.—A valuable accession. The deacons are Jesse Wood and Edwin Johnson. They support their minister by subscription.

The Quidnic Baptist meeting-house was built in 1808; it is 40 by 60 feet, having galleries, vestry, and 70 pews on the floor. It will seat 700 and is valued at only 1000, it being much out of repair. The congregation is 225, averaging 180. It has a debt of $200. The meeting-house lot is large and valuable. The deacon is Oliver Howard. This house is situated in the centre of a large population, and is such an important station that it should be immediately put in order. A generous individual has offered to contribute one half of the entire expense, if the other can be obtained.—This proposition will be submitted to the consideration of your Board of Managers by the pastor of this church.

The County of Kent according to the foregoing estimates has a population in the four towns that constitute it of 15,700; for whom there are provided 9,415 seats in public worship, at a valuation of $47, 700, with an aggregate property of $6,533,000. In this county there exist a large number of manufacturing interests, owned by residents in various places, but chiefly in

Providence and vicinity. These owners it may be do not realize their responsibilities to their operatives, or to the county at large. It will be of vital importance in their future account, (for every man shall give account of himself to God,) to have looked after not only their own pecuniary emolument, but also to the moral tone which they have given to society by the introduction of proper help into their manufacturing interests, and by the proper cultivation of their minds when thus located.

In this County their is ample room for the introduction of useful knowledge of every character, and for religious culture in the various villages, of which is is composed. In this county our ancestors evidently went to the other extreme in the moral education of their children. But let no one complain of the laws of Rhode-Island because they compel no one to perform religious homage contrary to his own wishes ; the fault lies not in the absence of legal merits, but in the want of a faithful parental culture. And further, we have all the law that necessity requires. For "all profaneness and immorality are furnished by the laws made to suppress them ; and while these laws are well executed, speculative opinions or modes of worship can never disturb or injure the peace of a State that allows all its subjects an equal liberty of conscience. Indeed it is not variety of opinions, or separation in worship, that makes disorders and confusions in government, for in both these there is great safety. But "it is the unjust, unnatural and absurd attempt to force all to be of one opinion, or to feign and dissemble that they are."

Providence County, incorporated in 1729.

I have already described two of the townships that were connected with this County at the time of its organization; viz. East Greenwich and Warwick. Providence in that year included the present County, save the town of Cumberland. In the following year Providence was divided into four townships, and since then its territory has been divided into nine towns, which with its own incorporation as a city, and the addition of Cumberland, make ten separate and distinct organizations. I proceed to give account of these in the same manner as I have done of the towns in the other counties.

PROVIDENCE in May, 1730, was formed into four townships, which were styled Providence, Smithfield, Glocester, and Scituate. Providence, by the repeated division of its boundaries, has become reduced to a small district, smaller than any other geographical assignment in the State. I shall defer an account of its present condition until I have completed the remaining nine.

CUMBERLAND denominated the "Gore of land" prior to the royal annexation of George II, was incorporated in January, 1746, and added to this county in the month following. It is the northern town; it has a population of 7000, and a property of $3,300,000. It contains a Universalist house, seating 500, and appraised at $8,000; two Methodist, accommodating 650, and valued at $8,500; a Roman Catholic, providing seats for 1,100, and an estate of $7,000; a Friend's, having room for 250 at a cost of 1,000; and three Associated Baptists.

The Woonsocket house, erected in 1833, measures 42 by 90 feet. It stands near the rail-road station, and is finished with a tower, bell, orchestra, vestry, 76 pews, and is valued at $6.000. It seats 500, the congregation being 400 and averaging 300; the population in the vicinity is 6.000. The pastor is sustained by rents of pews. They have no debt. The deacons have resigned and different persons officiate in the office. It is a very important field and is worthy of our continued affection; a child of the Convention, may the church never cease to own its relationship and to aid in the education of other children in like manner adopted.

The Cumberland Hill House, measuring 40 by 50 feet, was built in 1844, having 54 pews. It seats 300 persons, has a congregation of 125, averaging 90; it is finished with tower, bell, orchestra, vestries, is valued at $4.000, and is out of debt. Seventy families live within one mile of the premises. They have a fund for ministerial support amounting to $700, the interest of which with the pew rents and subscriptions they devote to this purpose. The deacon is Abner Ballou. There is in this region great room for improvement in temperance and Sabbath observance. Very many attend no religious services. The pastor speaks of four baptisms this year. The funds of the Convention can be well expended at this place until the ability of this abundantly able community can be drawn forth for the entire sustenance of the interest.

The Valley Falls house is situated in the Valley Village, on the Cumberland side. It was built in 1840, is 45 by 65 feet, and seats 400; it has a congregation of 200, averaging 150. It is furnished with a tower, bell, orchestra, organ, vestry, and 76 pews, at a cost of $7,000. A heavy debt of $5,000, and some ministerial arrearages, greatly depress the church. They report in both church and society, only about $24,000. The pastor is supported by rent of pews and subscription. The deacons are Amos Babcock and Otis Ingraham. Numerous removals from the village have occurred, and foreigners fill their places. It is hoped, however, that a change in this respect will be effected, and that the Board will in some manner enable them yet to retain their house.

SMITHFIELD was a division of Providence in May, 1730. It has a population of 12,000, and an estate of $1,100,000. There are three Episcopal houses, seating 1,100 at a cost of $18,000, (two Friends providing for 900, in valuation $2,500;) one Methodist, accommodating 225, and valued at $1,800 ; one Free Will Baptist, holding 480, at a cost of $1,200; two Congregationalists, seating 1500, at a valuation of $18,000 ; and three Associated Baptists.

Central Falls Baptist house seats 500, and is estimated at $7,000. It is a fine building, erected in 1844, measuring 45 by 65 feet, having a tower, bell, orchestra, organ, vestry and 76 pews, and is well located. The congregation is 400, averaging 300. The minister is sustained by pew rents and subscriptions. They have a debt of $250. The deacons are Preston Grant and German P. Thurber. It is a church of great promise. Rev. John Blain has become their pastor; he is greatly encouraged by the deep religious feeling existing among the people.

Lonsdale house was built in 1840, seats 400, and cost $3,000. It measures 40 by 50 feet, and is finished with tower, bell, organ, vestries and 58 pews. It has no debt. The congregation is 200, averaging 125. There is here a community of 1,100. The deacons are David Clark and W. Robinson. There is also an Episcopal house and a large foreign population in the vicinity. It is a manufacturing village of considerable note. Rev. W. Phillips, a brother beloved, supplies them. They sustain the ministry by pew rents.

Lime Rock and Albion house has provisions for 250 persons and is estimated at $1,500. It was erected in 1836, and measures 40 by 60 feet. It is situated on a hill some half mile from the village, and two miles from the Albion. It is believed that a removal of the house to the village below, would be the means of increasing the usefulness of the church. It has a tower, orchestra, and 50 pews, and is free from debt. The minister is maintained by subscription. There are more than 1,000 people in the vicinity. The congregation is 100, averaging 50. The deacon is Ebenezer Joe. Worship is held in the Albion village once on the Sabbath. Here there is a large agricultural, as well as manufacturing community. The people are wealthy, and ere long a new and independent interest should be sustained at both villages. Rev. D. M. Burdick of Tiverton has removed hither and become the pastor of this congregation.

Glocester, one of the first divisions of Providence, was incorporated in May, 1730, having a population of 3,000, and an estate of $1,000,000. There is a Congregational meeting-house, seating 328, at a cost of $3,500; an Union accommodating 211, and valued at $500; a Free Will Baptist, providing for 412, and valued at $3,800, and another society of the same denomination having no house but a congregation of 174.

Burrillville was separated from Glocester and made a township in October, 1806. It contains a population of 3,600 and $1,000,000 in property. There is a Free

Will Baptist meeting-house seating 300, at a cost of $3,000; a Methodist holding 250, and valued at $2,400; and a Friend's accommodating 250, at a valuation of $750.

SCITUATE, another portion of Providence, was constituted a township in May, 1730. It has a population of 5000, and property amounting to $1,900,000. The Census records one Congregational house, seating 400 and appraised at $2,000; two Free Will Baptists accommodating 750, with property at $3,500; one Millerite house providing for 250 and valued at $150; two Six Principle Baptist holding 450 and appraised at $2,000; and one Associated Baptist seating 200, and valued at $800. The latter is situated on a beautiful lot, between Jackson and Fiske villages It has a tower, bell, orchestra, and 52 pews. The church seems disheartened; indeed the Convention has never yet found much success at this station. Nevertheless for the present the church will hold a monthly meeting, and watch the movements of divine providence. The deacon is Benjamin Arnold who resides in the village of Phenix. There is a debt of $160, for which the premises are pledged. We may also add that there is in this town a Literary Institution, denominated the SMITHVILLE SEMINARY, which has always been under the direction of the Free Will Baptists; it furnishes advantages to all who desire to obtain a good English education. It is open to both sexes, without reference to any religious persuasion. Persons can also receive instruction in the Languages and classical studies.

FOSTER, formerly a part of Scituate, was made a township in August, 1781. It has a population of 2000 inhabitants and a property of $577,000. There are two Free Will Baptist Meeting-houses, the one seating 250 and valued at $1,200 the other accommodating 200, and in value $800.

CRANSTON, was the southern division of Providence as it remained after its incorporation in 1730. It was set off in June 1754. It has 7,000 inhabitants, and an estate of $2,223,000. There is a Friend's meeting-house seating 200 and in value $400; one Free Will Baptist, or South Benevolent Society accommodating 400, and appraised at $1,200; one Congregational said to seat 250, and in valuation $1,200; one Free Will Baptist, seating 200, and estimated at $600; and one Six Principle Baptist holding 500, and valued $1,200; and one Associated Baptist.

The house of the Associated Baptists is situated in the north part of Pawtuxet village, having been erected in 1803. It measures 38 by 50 feet, seats 400, has a congregation of 300 averaging 150, and is estimated at $1,200. It has a tower and bell, galleries and 71 pews on the floor. There are in the village 600 inhabitants. They sustain their minister by subscription, in the obtaining of which, and also for other services, they are under great obligation to the Rev. Job Manchester, a minister of the Six Principle Baptist order, and a resident in the village. The deacons are Remington Smith and Newell Lee. There is some special attention to religion prevailing in the congregation. They need a new house. The village has been greatly depressed, but there is great wealth among the residents and a brighter day evidently awaits them.

JOHNSTON, yet another division of Providence proper,

was incorporated in Febuary, 1759. Its population is 3,000, and its property $1,200,000. There are three houses of the Six Principle Baptist's, seating 1,500, and valued at $9,000; one Episcopal accommodating 400, and valued at $2,000; and one Free Will Baptist providing for 900, at a cost of $6,000, located in western Olneyville.

North Providence, the last division of Providence in 1730, was incorporated into a distinct township in June, 1765. The south part, bordering on and taking in some part of the compact town, and against which there was a powerful opposition at the time of its constitution, was again annexed to the town of Providence in June, 1767. It has a population of 8,000, and property in valuation $3,600,000. There is one Congregational house seating 600, and valued at $7,000; two Episcopal, holding 900, and estimated at $12,500; one Union, accommodating 280 and valued at $3,000; a Roman Catholic put down at 950, and appraised at $10,000; one Free Will Baptist, holding 250, and valued at $1,500; two Methodist providing for 800, at a cost of $5,000; and four Associated Baptists.

The High Street Baptist house is situated in Pawtucket village, measuring 56 by 64 feet, with an orchestra adjoining on the north, of 14 by 30 feet. It was built 1830; valuation $2,000. It seats 600, has a congregation of 300, averaging 150, and is finished with tower and bell, galleries and organ, vestry and 103 pews on the floor. It has also a large lot of land. The deacons are Olney Keach, Jabel Pall, Abner Polsy, and Pardon Allen. The Rev. A. Ross is at present preaching to them, and it is hoped the church which has been for some months scattered will now be gathered with a sure prospect of their permanent organization.

Near to the High Street stands the First Baptist Church, erected in 1842, at a cost of $11,000; it is free from debt. It measures 61½ by 91 feet. It will seat 900, has a congregation of 500, averaging 300; it is furnished with vestries and 114 pews on the floor, galleries and organ, tower and bell; from the rents of the pews with some subscription the pastor is sustained. The deacons are Daniel Dunham, George P. Jenks, Stephen Benedict, and James Olney. The house is substantial and ornamental. The Church is able and increasingly efficient. The field is large, numbering on both sides of the river 12.000 inhabitants.

The Fruit Hill house measures 30 by 60 feet. It was built in 1819, seats 300, and is valued at $2,000. It has 60 pews, with a congregation of 150, averaging 80. Rev, John C. Welch of Providence, a minister long and favorably known in Rhode Island as a pastor, supplies their pulpit; his labor is rewarded with tokens of good. This Church would probably increase their usefulness by the erection of a new house. The lot is large and finely situated, surrounded by the Fruit Hill village. A large agricultural district and several manufacturing interests furnish them with sufficient encouragement for such an enterprise. The Fruit Hill Classical School, taught by Stanton Belden Esq. is also here. Mr. Belden's reputation as a teacher has ever stood high; and the institution is worthy of a liberal patronage.

The Allendale Baptist Church was built in 1847, about three fourths of a mile south west from the Fruit Hill house. It is situated in the village of Zachariah Allen, Esq., a gentleman of high moral feeling, who contributes liberally towards the support of the church. The building measures 22 by 40 feet, has a tower, bell, vestry, and 27 pews, seats 250, and is estimated at $1,800. The church report their congregation at 300, with an average of 150. They sustain the ministry by subscription. Julius E. Johnson, an unordained minister, has supplied their pulpit on the Sabbath for two years. The deacon is Samuel C. Harrington. The population in the village is 300.

In the nine towns enumerated as belonging to Providence County there is a population of 50,600 inhabitants, for whom there are provided in houses of public worship 23,886 seats, with an estimated value in church property of $197.500, and with an aggregate of the personal property and landed estates of $20,000,000.

In six of these towns, embracing a population of 23,600, we have only the house at Fiskeville in Scituate, now closed, and the congregation in Pawtuxet village, in the extreme south-east of Cranston; in the large town of Smithfield with a population of 12,000, we are also but feebly represented, and the same can be said of Cumberland.

In five other towns in the State, containing a population of 5.900, we have no house of worship. Thus there are nine towns out of the thirty-one, having a population of 16,900 inhabitants, among whom there are no organizations of any kind connected with our denomination. And yet these towns are increasing at a rapid rate annually. With devout gratitude that christians of other denominations have carried the gospel to these sections, and with fervent prayer also that many, very many souls may be given to them for their reward, I would nevertheless remark that, if we as Baptists mean to survive and do justice to the providence that gave to us as a people these lands, we should devote our best energies and means, at least for a season, mainly to the improvement of the heart of our denominational body; and afterwards, having purified our moral blood and renewed our organic and muscular energy, we may be able to send forth moral life into other parts more effectually than we have ever done, and thus save ourselves from spiritual apoplexy, and aid also in preserving the souls of other people, and of the race at large, from the death that never dies.

The Township of Providence, as has been remarked, embraced originally the entire lands that are now embraced in Providence county, save the town of Cumberland, which before the settlement of 1746, was styled "The Gore of land." It was divided in May, 1730, and incorporated into four townships. It was lessened again in June, 1754, by the formation of Cranston; and in February, 1759, by the setting off of Johnston; and in June, 1765–7, by the establishment of North-Providence; leaving the boundaries in 1767 as they are at present described, viz; about 2½ miles in average breadth and about 3½ miles in average length. Thus Providence gave away eight towns, each larger than itself, contributing to Providencc County nine towns, which with Cumberland, make the ten towns, its present number. But notwithstanding it has thus furnished territory for all the large towns around, it has nevertheless nearly one third of the entire population of the State, and a number equal to all its immediate derivatives; about one third of the accommodations for public worship; and more than one third of the reported wealth or property. For, as is supposed, fifty-thousand people reside in the city proper, having 32,400 seats in houses of religious meetings, and representing $37,500,000:—statistics varying somewhat from those quoted by myself from the books to my teacher Liberty Rawson, Esq., when a boy at the Brick Free School-house in Meeting-street, forty years since, and ten years after the establishment of Free Schools in the State. At that time in 1810 Providence had a population of 10,071, and a property amounting to $3,509,000. Now she has a property amounting to $37,500,000, besides the vast estates held by her citizens within thirty miles, north, south and west, which include very much of the capital properties credited to the towns where they are located. Then the town tax was fifty-seven cents on one hundred dollars, in place of, under the city government, fifty-three cents, (this grand objection to a city government) when too the State had a population of 77,031, and not as now of 165,400; and a property of less than $30,000,000, in place of $91,375,000. In all probability the total amount of capital in Rhode Island for January, 1854, would equal if not exceed the sum of $100,000,000.

City of Providence incorporated in Oct. 1831.

The town of Providence became a city by an Act of incorporation passed by the General Assembly at their October session in 1831. Its first city officers were inducted into office in June, 1832. Gen. Samuel W. Bridgham became its first Mayor, retaining the office by repeated elections until December, 1839, when he died.

He was succeeded by Mr. Thomas M. Burgess, who officiated until 1852, when Mr. Amos C. Barstow was elected to the office. The present Mayor is Mr. Walter R. Danforth. The period of the town government of Providence has been one hundred and ninety-six years, and of the city government twenty-one years; making a total of two hundred and seventeen years since its settlement.

In February, 1800, mainly through the influence of the Association of Mechanics and Manufacturers in Providence, an Act was obtained from the General Assembly, establishing in the State a system of Free Schools; the town was divided into four districts and four schools were established, one in each district. And these great blessings were never withheld from the citizens, although the State law was repealed in February, 1703. In January, 1828, when the Public schools were re-established throughout the State by Legislative authority, Providence commenced its admirable system of Primary Schools in addition to those that had been continued and multiplied from 1800. In 1839 the whole system was revised and improved, and spacious brick houses were erected, which still remain an honor to the intelligence of its citizens, the true guarantee of civil rights, and the source of constant prosperity to the increasing population.

In this connection it is proper to mention the exceedingly useful Institution of the Society of Friends, established in 1819 and located in the north-eastern portion of the city on Hope street. At this institution the youth of both sexes receive a thorough education in all the branches of regular science, and in the languages.

The grounds are spacious, the buildings are large and commodious, and adequate means are furnished for exercise and other mediums of health and comfort. It is richly endowed by funds from estates of the late Obadiah Brown, and his father, Moses Brown; also by funds or donations from other benevolent patrons of the Society, by whom its concerns are managed through Trustees and Committees of their appointment, and to whom regular reports of its condition are made at its annual meetings. This and other schools of a high character having been founded by this very worthy christian people, the youth of their families have reaped great advantages.

In this city also, the University of the State is located. Its premises are bounded by Waterman, Brown, George and Prospect streets, thus forming an entire square with the exception of a private residence on the corner of Prospect and George streets. It was founded in 1764 and incorporated in February, of the same year.

"As early as the year 1707, the Philadelphia Baptist Association, composed of the Baptist Churches in that vicinity, was formed," having in view the prosperity of the denomination in America. Among other objects which that body favored, was an educated ministry. And as the colleges then existing were under severe restrictions of a sectarian character, and as candidates for their ministry were often subjected to great embarrassments, the plan was suggested to establish an institution for their own young men, the advantages of which however should be made equally free to persons of all religious persuasions. The distinct project of such an establishment in this State, is conceded to the Rev.

Morgan Edwards, a distinguished Baptist minister of Wales, who arrived in this country in 1761, and soon after settled in Philadelphia as Pastor of the First Baptist Church in that city. Immediately after the plan of a college was attempted, Mr. Edwards made very vigorous efforts both in this country and in England to obtain books for its library, and funds for its endowment; and he was mainly instrumental in obtaining its Charter. In 1762 the Philadelphia Baptist Association, having projected this institution, appointed Rev. JAMES MANNING, a recent graduate at Princeton, New Jersey, to visit Rhode Island and ascertain if this object would not receive the sympathies of the denomination in a State formed by men whose sentiments after its settlement had been developed as Baptist. In accordance with his instructions Mr. Manning visited Newport, and made known the plan and desires of the Association to the Governor and Deputy Governor residing in that town, and also to thirteen other gentlemen, all of whom were members of the Baptist churches then established in the place. From all of these gentlemen he at once received the most encouraging assurances. The question of the location of the College was the next in order. And as no funds had been raised, it seemed proper, at least in its beginning, that a town in which its presiding officer could officiate as pastor of a church, in order to secure in part a pecuniary support, would furnish the greatest security for the permanent success of the College. And as there were at that time some sixty Baptist communicants living in the town of Warren, who were members of Baptist Churches in Swansea, Newport, and elsewhere, it was decided by the above mentioned gentlemen, and the friends of the College generally, that Mr. Manning should take up his residence in that town, and become pastor of a church, which it was also proposed should be constituted by these Baptist communicants. Accordingly in the summer of 1764 Mr. Manning removed to Warren, and on the 15th of November ensuing, the Baptist Church in that place was formed, and he became its first pastor. The exercises were conducted by the Rev. Messrs. John Gano of New York, Gardner Thurston of Newport, and Ebenezer Hinds of Middleborough. The sermon was delivered by Mr. Gano. In September 1765, Mr. Manning was elected President of the College, and continued to exercise his collegiate and pastoral duties for more than five years in that town. On the 7th of September, 1769, the first Commencement was celebrated at Warren, and seven young men took the degree of Bachelor of Arts. Up to this period there had been no public edifice erected for the accommodation of the College. The exercises of Commencement awakened the sympathies of residents in many places in the Colony, who soon after that occasion, made applications to the Corporation for its permanent establishment within their boundaries. The towns of Warren, Providence, Newport, and East Greenwich, representing four counties of the State, all preferred their claims as presenting each respectively the most eligible situation. The towns of Providence and Newport were the two ablest competitors, the former offering a subscription of £4280, and the latter of £4000. February 7th, 1770, the Corporation by a vote of twenty-one to fourteen decided that the edifice should be built in Providence, and that there the College should be continued forever. Accordingly Mr. Manning removed to

Providence, and opened the institution in May, 1770, where all its exercises have since been held, with a temporary suspension only of some few years during the revolutionary war.

The University received its present name in honor of its most liberal benefactor, the late Hon. Nicholas Brown of Providence, by a vote of the Corporation passed September 6, 1804.

It will be seen from the foregoing statements that this University was projected and established by the Baptists, and that the Catholic spirit of its Charter was introduced because of the rigid sectarian character of the existing colleges. The College at first was in their own hands and might have remained under their control wholly. But under the circumstances they preferred that other denominations should be represented in the government of the institution. There were at that time when its Charter was granted, but four denominations of christians existing in the State, and from each of these a selection was made according to the numerical number of each. There were incorporated thirty-six Trustees, twenty-two of whom by the Charter, are to be forever Baptists; five to be of the denomination called Friends, or Quakers; four Congregationalists, and five Episcopalians. There is incorporated also another branch in the government, styled the Fellowship, consisting of twelve members, including the President, "eight of whom are to be Baptists, and the rest indefinitely of any or all denominations." The President must be a Baptist.

Among the provisions of the Charter is the following: "That into this liberal and Catholic institution shall never be admitted any religious tests: But on the contrary all the members hereof shall forever enjoy full, free, absolute and uninterrupted liberty of conscience: And that the places of Professors, Tutors, and all other officers, the President alone excepted, shall be free and open for all denominations of Protestants: And that youth of all religious denominations shall and may be freely admitted to the equal advantages, emoluments, and honors of the College or University: And that the public teaching shall, in general, respect the sciences; and that the sectarian differences of opinions shall not make any part of the public and classical instruction."

In 1850 material changes were made in the system of instruction given at this institution; the range of studies was greatly extended, and the sum of $125,000 (raised by subscription mostly among the citizens of Providence) was added to the College funds, thus augmenting them to about $200,000. The College Library contains upwards of 25,000 choice and well selected volumes, and the Libraries of the Philermenian and United Brothers Societies connected with the University contain 6000 additional volumes, making 32,000 volumes in all.

Brown University therefore, possessing ample college buildings, grounds, and funds, and having a large and excellent library, and being furnished with full supplies of apparatus in every department of science, and with competent instructers in ancient and modern learning, is adapted to the demands of a classical, mechanical, mercantile, moral, and physical education. From it have gone forth 1804 graduates, who have honored alike themselves and their Alma Mater in the various walks of professional life; a very large number of individuals have also received partial instruction at this seat of learning. The number of students or undergraduates now connected with the University is 283. From 1827, President Wayland has presided over its various interests; and during this period of twenty-eight years, a large number of gentlemen occupying the learned professions and other equally useful stations in New England and elsewhere, have received their moulding under his efficient and most admirable training.

This Institution has received the instructions of four Presidents. Its first, was its founder JAMES MANNING of Nassau Hall College, Princeton, who entered upon the duties of his office, September, 1765, and continued until his death, which occured at 4 o'clock, A. M., July 29th, 1791, at his own residence. He was succeeded by JONATHAN MAXCY of the class of 1787, who resigned in 1802, and who has since died. The same year, ASA MESSER of the class of 1790, was elected to the presidency; he resigned in 1826, and has since deceased. In 1827, FRANCIS WAYLAND, JR., of Union College, became its presiding officer.

No college has been conducted more faithfully on the principles recognized at its origin, than this. Young men of every religious persuasion, and even those who claimed to adhere to no persuasion whatever, have always found themselves perfectly at liberty to pursue their own views unrestricted by any undue influence from the Faculty of instruction. The discipline has always compared favorably with that of kindred colleges; and in no institution are greater advantages afforded to students in every department of useful learning than are tendered to youth in this, and that too without regard to their denominational or religious preferences.

At the eighty-fifth anniversary of the Warren Association, held in the town of Warren, Sept. 1 and 2, 1852, the twenty-second minute reads as follows, viz:

"The Rev. H. Jackson presented the following preamble and resolutions, which, after an animated discussion, participated in by the Rev. H. Jackson, J. N. Granger, B. Miner, R. A. Fyfe, T. C. Jameson and Dr. Wayland, were unanimously adopted, viz:

Whereas in the year 1764, the fathers of this Association met in this town, the town of Warren, and founded Rhode Island College, now denominated Brown University, and commended the Institution to the patronage of these and other churches; therefore,

Resolved, First, That we, the members of this Association in 1852, cordially respond to the call of those fathers, and strongly sympathize with them in the great interests of that venerable seat of learning.

Resolved, Second, That as the Warren Association at its first anniversary in the year 1767, eighty-five years ago this month, solemnly consecrated the College, then in its infancy, to Science and the Church, we in our place do, on this 2d day of September, 1852, solemnly and heartily renew the Covenant then written and confirmed. And therefore,

Resolved, Third, That we recommend this University to the deep sympathy and earnest prayers of the churches of the Father of our Lord Jesus Christ, the Great Head of the church, of whom the whole family in heaven and earth is named, that the young men, who there resort for an education, may be strengthened with might by his Spirit in the inner man, and that the Spirit of the heavenly Teacher may dwell in them by faith, and that they may be filled with *all* the fulness of God."

It will not be improper to remark in this connexion, that the cause of education had received considerable attention in the State at large prior to the established public schools in 1800, although there has never been made sufficient provision for the wants of the population. Nevertheless we should be grateful that previously to that period, there were academies in operation in all the counties, and in some of them, several, besides a large number of private schools.

In the returns of the State Commissioner, the Hon. E. R. Potter of Kingstown, for January, 1853, it appears that the population in the State under fifteen years old was in June, 1850, 47,357; and that of this number 28,331 attended school within that year, and that 2,744 could not read or write. That the whole number of scholars connected with the schools in 1852 according to the returns (several districts not reporting) received by him was 26,187, averaging in attendance 18,772; and that of these scholars 13,979 were males, and 12,208 were females. And that there were 263 male teachers and 345 female teachers, (608 teachers, furnishing to every teacher 43 scholars,) making a total of 26,798. Of the 47,857 youths under 15 years, 13,898 were not four years of age, leaving 33,959 over 4 and under 15. Of the 33,959 youths, 28,331 attended school, which leaves 5,628 not reported. Making only a reasonable allowance for incompetency by physical and mental inability, and for instruction obtained otherwise than in regular schools, and the result will show that the youth of our State are to a great extent receiving more or less education at school. It is confidently believed that under the present system of management, the number of scholars and of teachers will be increased; and that education both in character and extent will greatly improve.

The following gentlemen constitute the government of Brown University, 1853–4.

BOARD OF FELLOWS.

REV. FRANCIS WAYLAND, D. D. L L. D., PRESIDENT.

Rev. Nathan B. Crocker, D. D.
Rev. Robert E. Pattison, D. D.
Hon. John Pitman, L L. D.
Hon. Richard Fletcher, L L. D.
Hon. James H. Duncan, A. M.
John Carter Brown, A. M.
Rev. Alvan Bond, D. D.
Alexander Duncan, A. M.
Hon. Isaac Davis, L L. D.
Rev. James N. Granger, A. M.
John Kingsbury, A. M.

JOHN KINGSBURY, A. M., SECRETARY.
MOSES BROWN IVES, TREASURER.

BOARD OF TRUSTEES.

HON. JOHN BROWN FRANCIS, PRESIDENT.

*Hon. Tristam Burges, L L. D.
Sullivan Dorr,
Rev. David Benedict, D. D.
Moses Brown Ives, A. M.
Hon. Richard W. Greene, L L. D.
Richard J. Arnold, A. M.
Zachariah Allen, L L. D.
Hon. Tomas Burgess,
Rev. Rufus Babcock, D. D.
Rev. Henry Jackson, A. M.
Hon. Levi Haile, A. M.
Hon. Heman Lincoln,
Samuel Boyd Tobey, M. D.
Hon. Benjamin B. Thurston,
Rev. William Phillips, A. M.
Rev. William Hague, D. D.
Robert H. Ives, A. M.
Rev. Baron Stow, D. D.
Rev. Edward B. Hall, D. D.
Hon. Edward Mellen, A. M.
Nathan Bishop, A. M.
Rev. Alva Woods, D. D.
Rev. Thomas Vernon, A. M.
William A. Crocker, A. M.
Rev. Arthur S. Train, A. M.
Horatio N. Slater, A. M.
Rev. Samuel B. Swaim,
Hon. Samuel G. Arnold, A. M.
Hon. Thomas P. Shepard, M. D.
George Howland, A. M.
Hon. Charles Thurber, A. M.
Albert Day,
Rev. Sewall S. Cutting.

*Deceased October 13, 1853.

EXECUTIVE BOARD.

REV. FRANCIS WAYLAND, D. D. L L. D., CHAIRMAN.

Rev. Nathan B. Crocker, D. D.
Hon. John Pitman, L L. D.
Moses Brown Ives, A. M.
Samuel B. Tobey, M. D.
Rev. Alva Woods, D. D.
John Kingsbury, A. M.
John C. Brown, A. M.
Rev. James N. Granger, A. M.
Hon. Samuel G. Arnold, A. M.

JOHN KINGSBURY, A. M., Secretary of the Board.

COMMITTEE OF AWARD.

Rev. Francis Wayland, Moses B. Ives, John Kingsbury.

MEMBERS OF THE FACULTY, AND OTHER OFFICERS.

Rev. Francis Wayland, D. D., L L. D., *President*, and Professor of Moral and Intellectual Philosophy.

Rev. Alexis Caswell, D. D., *Regent*, and Professor ot Mathematics and Physical Astronomy.

George I. Chace, P. D., LL. D., Professor of Chemistry and Physiology, and of Chemistry applied to the Arts.

William Gammell, A. M., Professor of History and Political Economy.

John L. Lincoln, A. M., Professor of the Latin Language and Literature.

Rev. Robinson P. Dunn, A. M., Professor of Rhetoric and English Literature.

Samuel S. Greene, A. M., Professor of Didactics.

James B. Angell, A. M., Professor of Modern Languages.

Rev. Henry Day, A. M., Professor of Natural Philosophy and Civil Engineering.

Nelson Wheeler, A. M., Professor of the Greek Language and Literature.

William F. Webster, A. B., Assistant to the Professor of Chemistry.

Reuben A. Guild, A. M., Librarian.

Edward T. Caswell, A. B., Assistant Librarian.

Lemuel H. Elliott, Register.

In the city of Providence there are forty-eight religious congregations assembling on the Sabbath, representing fifteen denominations of professing christians, all existing on the voluntary principle in a State where, concerning religious compulsion, there has never been enacted in any form a law; but every citizen is recommended by his Excellency the Governor to offer thanksgiving upon his own acknowledged altar, and to observe God's holy day in a manner becoming, and in accordance with the requisitions of the Bible.

Of these forty-eight assemblies, four meet in public halls. To these several denominations are assigned their proportion of seats and their estimated value in the annexed table, viz:

Denominations.	Seats.	Valuation.
Associated Baptists,	6,300	$179,700
Orthe. Congregationalists,	5,975	148,200
Roman Catholics,	5,150	98,(·00
Methodist Episcopal,	3,365	61,800
Episcopalians,	3,150	110,000
Unitarian Congregationalists,	2,350	118,000
Universalists,	1,450	53,200
Christians,	1,000	12,000
Free Will Baptists,	1,000	10,000
Mariners' Church,	700	4,500
Wesleyan Methodists,	500	6,000
Society of Friends,	500	20,000
Second Adventists,	400	——
Associated Scotch Pres.,	300	3,000
New Jerusalem,	250	4,000
Total of Seats and Valuation,	32,400	$829,700

There are therefore in this city in the forty places of public worship 32,400 seats, and $829,700 property in church premises, being full one half of the pecuniary investments of this character in the State, and as I have before stated nearly one third of the pew accommodations.

Of these forty-eight meetings, there are seven Orthodox Congregational, four Roman Catholic, six Methodist and Episcopal, four Episcopal, three Unitarian Congregational, two Universalist, two Christian, four Free Will Baptist, one Mariner, one Wesleyan Methodist, one Society of Friends, two Second Advent, one Scotch Presbyterian, one New Jerusalem, and nine Associated Baptists.

The First Baptist Church is the representative of the first individuals who were publicly baptized by immersion in America, the original church having consisted, in part of the organization thus formed in 1638-9;—and it has continued until the present time in the neighborhood where Williams and his associates were immersed.

And so universally received has been this impression that Callender, our oldest historian places it first in order, and the Legislature as late as May, 1774, grants a charter in which they say it is "the oldest Christian Church in this Colony," and hence in existence first, and before any other church of whatever profession, within their jurisdiction.

In relation to the division in this church in 1652-3, the Rev. John Comer is the only author that I have seen who has given any particular account of that event. Backus, Benedict and Staples quote from him all that they have stated respecting it. Nor does Hopkins give any other authority. The records of the Providence church, it is said, are not sufficiently accurate to decide the question authoritatively; nor according to Backus, Vol. II, Page 3, are the records of the church in Newport in much better condition, for as he writes, this "church had but seventeen members when he, Mr. Comer, "came there, in 1726; neither had they any church records before he got a book and collected into it the best accounts that he could obtain of their former affairs." Who then was Mr. Comer? He was born in Boston, August 1st, 1704; baptized in that town January 31st, 1725; settled as pastor of the First Baptist Church in Newport, May 19th, 1726; dismissed from his pastoral office January 8th, 1729; preached as a supply for nearly two years in the Second Baptist Church in Newport; settled as pastor of the Baptist Church in Rehoboth January 26th, 1732; and died of consumption in that town, May 23d, 1734, aged 29 years, 9 months and 22 days. He was a gentleman of education, piety, and of great success in his profession.

During his brief life he collected a large body of facts, intending at some future period to write the history of the American Baptist Churches. His manuscripts he never printed, nor did he as I learn ever prepare them for publication. He was unable to revise them, and they were left in their original condition. Nevertheless he made an able and most valuable contribution to Rhode Island history. His papers were written probably about the year 1729, or in 1731. The Rev. John Callender, his successor in the Newport Church, was settled Oct. 13th, 1731. He was a contemporary with Mr. Comer, and in all probability also an intimate correspondent. As Mr. Comer united with the church in Boston, of which Rev. Elisha Callender, an uncle of the Newport pastor, was the minister, and as they even resided together at the same time in Newport, the writings of Comer must have been well known to Mr. John Callender. And especially, inasmuch as while he was preparing his Century Sermon in 1738, he must have had access to them and indeed to all sources from which Comer had derived his knowledge of the events which he described. And yet Mr. Callender in that discourse does not intimate, as Mr. Comer is made to say, that the church in Providence of which Mr. Wickenden was an elder, was a new church; and that the church in that same place of which Mr. Olney was pastor, was the original body organized there in 1639; but he states simply, that "about the year 1653-4 there was a division in the Baptist Church at Providence, about the right of laying on of hands." Hereupon they walked in two churches, one under Mr. C. Browne, Mr. Wickenden, &c., the other under Mr. Thomas Olney." The question here arises, which of these two bodies was in the opinion of Mr. Callender the original church? This he does not decide, and yet when he wrote that discourse four years after Mr. Comer's death, he was possessed of all the information which Mr. Comer had obtained, and was better qualified to give an opinion, for he employed six months for revision and still further researches;—and to use his own language in his dedication article, "I hope there are few or no errors in the matters of fact related, or the dates that are assigned. To prevent any mistakes, I have carefully reviewed the public records, and my other materials; this review has brought to my knowledge or remembrance, many things that were not mentioned in the pulpit, which however it seemed ought not to be omitted." And had he believed that the Newport Church was the first in America, he never would have placed that at Providence in the position in which he has. His order in the arrangement is peculiar. He places Mr. Olney's church as second, "one under Mr. C. Browne, Mr. Wickenden, &c., the other under Mr. Thomas Olney; but laying on of hands at length generally obtained." "This last continued till about twenty years since, when becoming destitute of an elder, the members were united with other churches. At present, there is some prospect of their re-establishment in church order." Evidently Mr. Callender had in his mind the existing church from the beginning of its organization in 1639; for he continues his history of it in the next paragraph save one. "*This Church* that out into divers branches, &c.," referring to the same body, which he began to describe in page 109, (Elton's Callender;) nor did he stop after he had informed us of the ceasing of the Olney church in 1718, but continued the history of the church " under Mr. Browne, Wickenden, &c.," till he came to account for the rise of the Newport church on pages 116-17, of the same edition. The history of Callender is therefore in my judgment, the history of the First Baptist Church existing in Providence from 1639 until his times;—and this church will, it is believed, continue to be a Baptist church to serve successive generations who will require the same gospel which their fathers loved while living, and triumphed in while dying.

For myself I do not question that had Comer lived until 1739, he would have sympathized with Mr. Callender entirely in the chronology of these and other churches, and of the various events of which the latter has so calmly, and cautiously, and judiciously written; a production, concerning which Judge Staples has said, " no publication of the kind deserves higher praise for impartiality, candor, and research."

As to Mr. Olney we have no knowledge of his ordination. It is recorded that in 1642, Chad. Browne was ordained an elder in the Providence Church. At a subsequent period, while together in New York, it is also recorded that Mr. Browne ordained Mr. William Wickenden to the same ministry. Gregory Dexter was also an elder in the same church before the division in 1652. Olney, Brown, and Wickenden, were members of the community concerning whom Gov. Winthrop said, " Mr. Williams and the rest did make an order that no man should be molested for his conscience;" and who in their own code prescribed " only in civil things," would they be governed by legal enactments. And Wickenden, Olney and Dexter were members of the first General Assembly at Portsmouth in May, 1647. At the time of the division before referred to, there were four elders in that church, viz: Chad. Browne, William Wickenden, Gregory Dexter, and Thomas Olney. Is it not probable that as *three* of these remained in the one, and only *one* of them in the other, that the former, although they did introduce a new ceremony into the church, were the majority of the original church, and the latter the minority? For with the former there are connected whatever records which are in existence, and to it also Callender, Hopkins, Backus, and Benedict refer as being the First Baptist Church in Providence. Indeed they never intimate that it was not the original church, even with the writings of Comer in their hands. Callender assuredly wrote of both these churches and also of the one at Newport, and he said that the church in Providence was first in order; nor does he give room for any suspicion that the one existing in that town in 1738, was not the original body. Certainly had there been any doubt in his mind, he would not in that year, twenty years subsequent to the disbandment of the Olney church, have chronicled the church then in being, as the Baptist Church in Providence from the days of Williams, and the first in order in our denomination in this country. In addition to the fact that no early reference to the church of Mr. Olney is found in print save that which Callender has made, viz: that it ceased in 1718 to be a church, and that its members sought membership in other churches, the unanimous voice of Baptists and others has awarded to the First church the claim which generation after generation has been compelled to allow, viz: that of priority. And is it not impossible that this claim can be otherwise than just, when Callender, although he had been in communion and conversation with Comer, presents notwithstanding a version of the case, destitute of the main discrimination of the manuscript writings of the latter? And is it not probable that if Mr. Comer had been living in 1738, with the revision and research of his writings and attainments which Callender gave to his preparations, these two men of Newport distinguished in Baptist history and Baptist principles, would have united in their testimony, that the church formed at the baptism of Williams, has come down in regular descent, thus making the *First Baptist Church in Providence in March* 1854, TWO HUNDRED AND FIFTEEN YEARS OLD?*

The former edifice of the existing church stood on the north side of Smith, corner of Smith and North Main streets; the one which they now occupy was erected in 1776, in the centre of a beautiful and almost oblong square, about two hundred by three hundred feet, bounded by North Main, Thomas, Benefit, and President streets. It is surrounded by an open fence, with neat walks of brick laid from its gate ways through the green surface to the various doors of the house, made on each side of the square, so that it can be vacated in the least time of any building of its size among us. The house is eighty feet square, with an addition of 16 feet,

*The venerable Stephen Hopkins, for eight years Governor of the Colony, but who is better known as one of the signers of the declaration of independence, in his account of Providence published in 1765, (See Mass. Hist. Col. 2d series, vol. 9) states as follows. "This first church of Baptists, at Providence, gathered and formed some time earlier than 1639, hath from its beginning kept itself in repute, and maintained its discipline, so as to avoid scandal, or schism, to this day; hath always been, and still is a numerous congregation, and in which I have with pleasure observed, very lately, sundry descendants from each of the above named founders, except Holliman."

thus making it 96 by 80 feet. It has a steeple 212 feet high. It is built of wood, and is furnished with galleries, vestries, bell, clock, and organ. There are 144 pews on the floor. The building is a noble structure, and seems to hold its superiority in symmetry of architecture, simplicity of design, and beauty of execution, notwithstanding the various attempts made at different times to excel it. And it is most ardently desired that no effort on the part of the society will be withheld to preserve it for many years to come in its firmness and strength. The architect was Joseph Brown, the builder, T. Sumner. In this house from its first opening, the college in Providence has held its annual commencements ; and on these occasions we should sigh after commencement were it not celebrated, even as we did when the anniversary of Brown was celebrated upon one sad Wednesday in July, instead of on the good old first Wednesday in September, at 9½ of the clock, A. M. But the original day has been restored ; not so we fear this house would be restored should it by fire or otherwise be destroyed. Indeed it was in reality an emanation from the college, for it would never have been built, had not the Browns and others erected it in part for the accommodation of the college.

The whole premises, together with parsonage and some funds of the Society, at census valuation, are appraised at $100,000. The house seats 1500, congregation 900, average 600.

This church has long been distinguished for the benevolence of its members, and at numerous times has enjoyed precious revivals of religion. From age to age it has stood a monument to the truth ; and distant may that day be, when its influence and its benevolence shall in any measure be lessened. The deacons are N. Bump, V. J. Bates, J. H. Read, W. Andrews, and M. Lyon. The minister is sustained by taxes upon the pews.

More than a century and an half had elapsed, and about thirty years after the erection of the house of the First church, before the Second, or Pine st. church, was organized. In 1805 a colony from the mother church was constituted a church, and an edifice was erected, which was carried away by the flood and gale of the 23d of September, 1815. In that house of blessed memory, many treasures were laid up by Cornell and Gano, between whom as pastors beloved, there subsisted an unbroken fellowship and sympathy in labor, yet to be brought forth,—for Jehovah neither confines himself to houses made with hands, nor loses his redeemed, if the outer sanctuary be destroyed. The following year, 1816, and on the same site, the present structure, excepting an enlargement in 1837, was erected, measuring 50 by 90 feet, with a tower and bell, galleries and organ, vestries and 106 pews. It is capable of seating 900 and is valued at $10,000. A debt of $1000 remains. It stands on the corner of Dorrance street, fronting on Pine, from which latter street it took its name.

This church has enjoyed many refreshings from the presence of the Lord. It is a valuable body, and if their present effort succeeds to build in a better location another edifice, which they greatly need, and towards which more than $20,000 have already been subscribed, we may expect even greater aid to the cause of truth than they have hitherto given. The deacons are W. Ham, B. Gardner, J. J. H. Butler, and J. Boyce. Their minister they sustain by rents of pews. Their congregation is 500, averaging 400.

Sixteen years had passed away before another Baptist Church was formed. George Dodds, whose memory can never be forgotten, residing at the time in the south-eastern section of the town, deeply interested in the spiritual condition of his neighbors and other citizens, by untiring perseverance in penny collections and journeys abroad, obtained means to erect the Third Baptist Meeting-house in 1822. It is situated on a large lot, on the corner of Wickenden and Hope streets; it was enlarged in 1838. It measures 45 by 71 feet, and has a tower and orchestra, extending its length to 93 feet. It is furnished with bell, organ, galleries, and vestries, has 92 pews on the floor, and is valued at $14,000. It will seat 900, has a congregation of 600, averaging 400. They support their minister by pew rents and subscriptions. The deacons are W. C. Barker, J. Luther, N. Mason, S. Barker, S. S. Stillwell and I. Goddard: The church was constituted in 1821.

This church is an efficient body of believers, distinguished for their liberality and the spiritual character of their social meetings; the influence which they exert is decidedly beneficial, Their pastor the Rev. T. C. Jameson, was settled in 1840, and resigned his office on the evening of the 3d of November, having performed a highly useful ministry of thirteen years among them.

Between Wickenden street and the First Church there is a position which ought long before now to have been occupied by our denomination.

Two years from the date of the Third, (i. e. 1823) the Fourth Baptist Church was constituted, their house having been erected in 1822. It is built on Bacon street, in the north part of the city, and measures since its enlargement in 1850, 47 by 74 feet; it is valued at $8,500. It has a tower and bell, orchestra and organ, chapel and vestries, and 92 pews on the floor. It seats 600, and has a congregation of 500 with an average attendance of 300. They support the ministry by rents and taxation of pews. They have two deacons, Cyril Babcock and Luther Salisbury.

This is also a valuable and efficient church. Their pastor, the Rev. Francis Smith, was settled in 1841, and resigned in October 1853, after a ministry of twelve years, during which he often witnessed tokens for good.

Seventeen years after the date of the Fourth Church, (i. e. in 1840,) the Fifth Baptist was formed. Their house now located on Stewart street, in the south-west section of the city, was built in 1845; it measures 38 by 60 feet, has 80 pews, and seats 500; it has a congregation of 300, averaging 150, and is valued at $1,600. They rent their pews. The deacons are, W. H. Hudson, G. Burr, B. Orswell, and H. C. Starkweather.

Rev. B. Miner, pastor of the South church has preached for them on Sabbath afternoons, they worshipping in the morning with his people. The members appear disheartened, but it is hoped that they will soon unite with the South church in the erection of a new house. Already something like $10,000 have been subscribed for this object. It is believed, that these two churches united in one, will be a blessing to that part of the city, rapidly increasing as it is in population and influence.

During the year 1840, the Meeting street church was also constituted, they occupying a house built in 1820 for the benefit of the colored population. It is 40 by 50 feet, and is finished with orchestra, 52 pews, and vestry, the whole being valued at $5000. It will accommodate 400; the congregation is 80, averaging 60. It stands on Meeting street, whence the church derives its name. The deacons are G. C. Willis, Z. Jones, and G. Waterman. The minister is sustained by subscription. Having no pastor, their pulpit is supplied by Bro. J. Amos. It is desirable that the members cultivate a deep interest in each other, and as they have no debt, there is no reason, provided they obtain a pastor and continue in prayer, why they should not prosper. The colored population is very large in the city. This church have invited Bro. C. Leonard to become their pastor. *

Six years after the Fifth, (i. e. in 1847) the South church was organized. The meeting-house which they occupy is the private property of Dea. E. S. Barrows. It is situated on Point street, and measures 33 by 70 feet, has a tower, orchestra, organ, 80 pews, and vestries, and is valued at $3,000. It will seat 400, has a congregation of 200, with an average of 125. They bear their expenses from pew rent and subscription. The deacons are T. Reynolds and E. S. Barrows. They have a flourishing Sabbath school, and with continued effort it is confidently believed that they will be able, in conjunction with the Fifth church, to erect a suitable edifice upon a lot already purchased. Such a house will be an important acquisition to the people.

The year following 1847 the Eighth church was established. They meet in their house, situated on the corner of Davis and Common streets; it was built in 1846, measures 35 by 50 feet, has 56 pews, and will seat 300. It is valued at $1,600. Their congregation is

* Rev. Mr. Leonard was ordained as their pastor, December 1853.

200, with an average of 150. They rent their pews. The deacons are E. Whipple and W. G. Noyes. About 180 families live in their vicinity, and their church and the Catholic, are the only houses for religious worship in the neighborhood. The interest is prosperous and well deserves the sympathies of the Convention. There is a prospect of great good from this station.

Five years after the formation of the Eighth, the Ninth. or High-street Baptist church was constituted ; the house is on Stewart street, corner of Pond, and measures 56 by 91 feet. It was dedicated in 1852. It is built of brick in the most substantial manner, is ornamented with two towers of the same materials, contains 134 pews, and is furnished with bell, orchestra and organ, vestry, study, and library rooms ; it is finished in neat yet elegant style, and is in reality a great addition to the public buildings of the city. It seats 800 ;—the congregation is 700, averaging 500. The cost ($36,000) has been met by Perry Davis, a recently ordained minister in the church, who I am informed, has said that the church shall not fail to enjoy it as their permanent place of public worship. The deacons are P. Davis, J. Davol, B. P. W. Bennett, and D. W. Robinson. This church united with the Providence Baptist Association at its last session.

The edifice is plain and yet in some respects quite ornamental. It is more entirely finished than any church within my knowledge. The audience room is very imposing, and the whole structure is rarely excelled in simplicity, conveniences, and durability. May a kind providence succeed the desires of the generous builder, and accept at his hands this monument to His praise.

ESTIMATES OF THE FIVE COUNTIES, 1854.

Counties.	Churches.	Church Prop.	Seats.	Population.	Valuation.
Newport,	44	$240,950	17,206	22,300	$14,500,000
Washington,	47	105,500	14,305	17,600	6,822,000
Bristol,	11	104,350	6.720	9,200	6,000,000
Kent,	32	48,200	9,615	15,700	6,553,000
	134	$499,000	47,846	64,800	$38,875,000
Providence Co.					
Nine towns,	58	$197,500	23,886	50,600	$20,000,000
City,	48	829,700	32,400	50,000	37,500,000
Total in R. I.,	240	$1,526,200	104,132	165,400	$91,375,000

Some of these estimates may be low, but others again are full high, so that the facts I think will compare with the various computations. Indeed I differ very slightly from the United States census as reported in 1850, excepting in cases where I know changes have taken place. By that census the population returned from the State of Rhode-Island was 147,545 ; the above estimate, aside from Providence, in which there is an increase of 8,487, increases it 9,368, making at the commencement of 1854, a population of 165,400, with church accommodations for 104,132. The late census makes the aggregate of property $80,508,794 ; in the table above it is augmented $10,855,206; of this increase $6,834,650 are rated in the tax books of our cities, Newport and Providence, making, with an additional increase of $4,031,556, for the State at large, the present capital of the State, $91,375,000. The property in church investment as rendered in the census of 1850, was $1,252,900 ; in this report, in consequence of additions of new churches and enlargement of former buildings, it is increased $273,300. I therefore state this investment at $1,526,200.

It will appear from the table following, that fifty-one of the two hundred and forty churches in Rhode-Island, are connected with the Rhode-Island Baptist State Convention. The year in which each of these churches was constituted, so far as has been ascertained, is given. Also the names of the pastors and clerks; the time also when the pastor was settled, and the compensation which he receives. This compensation amounts in the aggregate to the sum of $21,942, thus averaging in the forty-three salaries received, per minister $510—hardly a common clerk's wages.—The whole membership of the churches as stated in the table annexed is 7124, of whom 2066 are males, and 5058 are females ; of the males 484 are reported as living in other places, and of the females 983. From this table it will also appear that in addition to their ordinary expenses, there has been raised in these churches during the current year for benevolent purposes the sum of $13,460,45, not $2000 of which has been expended upon Rhode-Island, loudly as our interests call for aid;—thus more than $11,000 have gone abroad; also that there are numbered in their respective congregations of worship 15,695 persons; and that the average attendance on the Sabbath in *ordinary weather* is 9,685. But it should be remembered that every church has members of other churches in its congregation, hence it may be inferred, that the actual church membership in each congregation is about what is here reported.

Names of Regular Baptist Churches, Pastors and Clerks in R. I., 1853.

Churches.	Pastors.	Clerks.	Churches, when constituted.	Pastors, when settled.	Salary of Ministers.	Male Members.	Female Members.	Total.	Males Absent.	Females Absent.	Moneys raised in 1853 for Benevolent purposes.	Congregation.	Average Congregation.
Warren, ...		H. Sanders, ...	1764		$1,000	61	197	258	12	18	$550	750	500
Bristol, ...	I. N. Hobart, ...	N. B. Cook, ...	1811	1852	600	27	90	117	7	22	132	400	150
Central, Tiverton, ...		T. Osborn, ...	1850		300	10	25	35	2	3	17 28	200	90
New Shoreham, ...	C. C. Lewis, ...	A. Dodge, ...	1780	1851	400	87	144	231	6	6		300	150
†First, Newport	S. Adlam, ...	B. B. Howland, ..		1849	600	95	230	325	7	17	250	700	450
Second, Newport, ...	J. O. Choules, ...	G. C. Shaw, ...	1656	1847	*800	60	158	218	17	22	300	600	350
Central, Newport, ...	H. Jackson, ...	D. C. Denham, ...	1847	1847	*800	57	175	232	3	7	400	700	450
East Greenwich, ...	—— Warren, ...	J. C. Harris, ...	1839	1853	600	15	105	120	4	20	15	250	150
N. Kingston, Quoitnessit, ...	W. Allen, ...	J. L. Congdon, ...	1839	1851		55	84	139	23	34		200	125
N. Kingston, Wickford, ...	J. E. Chesshire, .	N. N. Spink, ...	1834	1852	600	37	87	124	2	4	185	300	160
First, N. Kingston, ...	J. A. Tillinghast,	J. Eldred, ...	1782	1853	300	55	124	179	12	8	100	300	150
First, S. Kingston, ...	J. M. Church, ...	D. M. C. Steadman	1788	1853	600	102	167	269	18	26	100	600	400
Second, S. Kingston, ...	J. P. Burbank, ..	W. S. Browning, .	1843	1851	125	29	38	67	10	19	20	150	95
Charlestown, ...	J. P. Burbank, ..	J. W. Taylor, ...	1840	1851	50	38	39	77	20	21	10	100	75
Westerly, Niantic, ...		B. Potter, ...	1851		50	10	8	18	1	1	80	100	60
Westerly, Lot. Village, ...		E. Pendleton, ...	1848			10	21	31	4	9		150	25
Westerly, First, ...	F. Denison, ...	A. Bull, ...	1835	1847	*600	85	194	279	21	54	147	450	300
Hopkinton, First, ...		H. M. Wells, ...	1834			22	28	50	4	6		60	40
Hopkinton, Second, ...	S. B. Bailey, ...	A. G. Nichols, ...	1841	1849	350	80	177	257	13	39	50	300	150
Richmond, Second, ...	G. K. Clark, ...	A. S. Kenyon, ...	1723	1849	100	25	55	80	15	33	50	80	50
S. Kingston, Queen's River, ..		I. T. Hopkins, ...	1819	1843		31	53	84	11	19		125	60
Exeter, ...	B. Johnson, Jr.,	C. G. Green, ...	1750	1837		69	121	190	23	52	21	250	100
West Greenwich, ...	J. Tillinghast, ...	J. P. Stone, ...		1840		40	89	129				100	50
Warwick and E. Greenwich, ..	I. Bates, ...	D. H. Wightman,	1743	1849		30	50	80	5	12		200	75
Coventry, Central, ...	A. Sheldon, ...	C. Whipple, ...	1853	1842	400	27	51	78	8	13	50	400	200
Coventry, Quidnic, ...	J. Brayton, ...	E. Andrews, ...	1851	1850	450	8	20	28	2	6	206	225	180
Warwick, First, ...	J. Brayton, ...	R. M. Bennett, ...	1805	1850	200	29	50	79	12	25	180	175	75
Warwick, Lippitt & Phœnix, ..	B. F. Hedden, ...	W. B. Spencer, ...	1842	1851	450	63	207	270	37	83	225 50	300	165
Warwick, Natic, ...	S. A. Thomas, ...	H. A. Bowen, ...	1839	1852	426	25	82	107	11	31	76	275	200

Warwick, Showomet,........	G. A. Willard,..	J. W. Greene,....	1842	1851	275	6	21	27	2	5	40	14	100	80
Cranston, Pawtuxet,.........	G. Peirce,.......	R. Smith,........	1805	1851	400	12	55	67	5	16	38		300	150
Scituate, Fiskville,..........	————	E. Read,.........	1829	————	————	8	52	60	————	————	————		————	————
N. Providence, Allendale,....	————	J. H. Vincent,....	1850	1852	156	13	48	61	7	18	————		300	150
N. Providence, Fruit Hill,....	————	B. A. Whipple,...	1818	1852	260	10	36	46	2	————	70	74	150	80
Cumberland, Woonsocket,...	J. B. Breed,.....	W. Everett,......	1840	1852	600	22	120	142	2	10	201		400	300
Cumberland Hill,............	F. Wiley,.......	A. Ballou,.......	1841	1852	400	9	59	68	5	24	————		125	90
Cumberland, Valley Falls,...	G. Silver,.......	C. Lawton,.......	1832	1853	450	25	60	85	9	12	15		100	150
Smithfield, Lonsdale,........	————	W. P. Walsworth,	1840	1853	400	8	24	32	7	13	16		100	125
Smithfield, Lime Rock & Alb'n	D. M. Burdick,..	T. Mann,........	1835	1853	450	3	19	22	2	3	10		100	50
Smithfield, Central Falls,....	J. Blain,........	S. S. Mallery,....	1844	1853	500	40	85	125	6	16	83	55	400	300
N. Prov., H. st., Pawtucket,..	A. A. Ross,.....	J. Hood,.........	1838	1853	500	40	116	156			————		300	150
N. Prov., Pawtucket, First,..	E. Savage,......	N. Bates,........	1805	1853	900	64	169	233	10	20	450		500	300
Providence, Fourth,.........	————	G. B. Peck,......	1823	————	800	42	139	181	12	31	614	51	500	300
Providence, Eighth,.........	W. Randolph,...	H. R. Greene,....	1847	1852	550	18	40	58	3	5	105	51	200	150
Providence, High st.........	G. R. Darrow,...	D. W. Robertson,	1851	1851	700	61	81	142	6	10	156		700	500
Providence, Fifth,..........	————	A. N. Arnold,....	1840	————	500	38	87	125	12	35	29	75	300	150
Providence, South,..........	B. Miner,.......	L. Towne,........	1846	1850	600	20	34	54	2	2	————		200	125
Providence, Second,.........	S. W. Field,.....	E. I. Ham,.......	1805	1850	1000	81	226	307	15	12	700		500	400
Providence, Third,..........	————	J. H. Ormsbee,...	1821	————	1000	141	317	458	50	75	505	47	600	500
Providence, Meeting st.,.....	C. Leonard,.....	W. J. Brown,....	1840	1853	300	12	38	50	4	16	12		80	60
Providence, First,...........	J. N. Granger,...	E. M. Snow,.....	1639	1853	*1400	111	363	474	13	50	7248		900	600
		*And Parsonage.			$21942	2066	5058	7124	484	983	$13460	45	15795	9735

† In regard to the date of the First Church in Newport, the following extract from the second page of Mr. Comer's manuscript "History of the Baptists in Newport," may be appropriately added in this connection. The History itself may be found among the Backus Papers in the Cabinet of the Rhode Island Historical Society.

"Mr. Clarke attempted and by the help and blessing of Christ gathered and constituted a Church maintaining the doctrine of efficacious grace, and professing the baptizing of only visible believers upon personal profession by a total immersion in water—This was done as near as can be gathered about the year 1644, six years after founding the colony, although the first certain record of this honorable and religious action bears date Oct. 12, 1648, at which time it consisted of 12 members in full and visible church communion, who it is provable are the first constituent members who first covenanted solemnly to walk with God and with each other in particular church order and fellowship."

On page 10 Mr. Comer adds further in regard to this Church in Newport:—"Thus I have briefly given some account of the first settlement and progress of the first Baptist Church on Rhode Island in New England, and the first in America." Had Comer lived to revise his manuscripts, this singular and as it seems to me erroneous statement would have been corrected. For an account of Comer the reader is referred back to page 80. For a full account of the origin of the First Baptist Church in Providence, in the year 1639, five years previous to the formation of the above mentioned Church in Newport, the reader is also referred back to pages 13 to 22, and 79 to 85.

Of fifty-one churches in the State, from each of whom you have now heard, about one half have received pecuniary encouragement from this Convention ; and several of them, but for this body, would never have been constituted. And we need no better channel through which to effect even the largest desires of our hearts concerning our State. As you have seen, there are nine towns of our thirty-one, in which we have no church of our order, and nine of the remaining twenty-two, in which we are feebly represented. Our entire northwestern section, and to a great extent, our western also, where Baptist sympathies are so prevalent, we have never cultivated. There are thriving villages existing and coming into existence annually, in which we can and ought to establish churches. There are six places especially in which we must operate immediately, or our opportunity will cease. There are also, large tracts of agricultural districts, where no special effort is being made for the salvation of men. There is little appreciation of the Sabbath, and a great lack of responsibility, among even some of the members of our churches. Indeed, to a fearful extent, church relationship and privileges are not valued. In some of the churches, deeply rooted prejudices exist against any improvement in efficient piety. In almost all of them, there is a worldly spirit prevailing to an extent truly ominous of evil. An increase of riches is the concern of the day, so that the most fine gold has become dim indeed.

The following schedule shows the proportion of seats which each denomination in the State furnishes,with their estimated value. It must be remembered, that mostly census reports are given, for it would be difficult to allow for rise in property in the several locations since 1850. And besides, this standard is equally just to each of these bodies :—

DENOMINATIONS.	Seats.	Valuation.	Newport County, Churches, number of.	Washington County, Churches in.	Bristol County, Churches in.	Kent County, Churches in.	Nine Towns in Providence County, Churches in.	City of Providence, Churches in.	Total of Meeting Houses and Churches in Rhode Island.
Associated Baptist,.....	24.880	$363.300	5	14	2	9	12	9	51
Orthordox Congregatn'l,	13.053	241.550	4	1	2	2	6	7	22
Methodist Episcopal,....	9.920	123.500	3	3	2	2	6	6	22
Episcopalian,..........	12.206	252.500	7	5	2	3	6	4	27
Roman Catholic,........	9.600	151.200	2	—	1	1	2	4	10
Society of Friends,.....	6.370	56.900	6	4	—	2	5	1	18
Free Will Baptist,......	6.962	44.350	5	4	—	3	11	4	27
Six Principle Baptist,...	5.805	23.450	—	5	—	8	6	—	19
Christians,............	3.150	28.200	5	1	1	—	—	2	9
Unitarian Congregatn'l .	3.050	127.000	1	—	—	—	—	3	4
Seventh Day Baptists,..	3.100	20.000	1	7	—	—	—	—	8
Universalist,...........	1.950	61.200	—	—	—	—	1	2	3
Mariner's Church, ...	700	4.500	—	—	—	—	—	1	1
Color'd Church, reported	670	3.300	2	2	1	—	—	—	5
Second Adventists,.....	650	150	—	—	—	1	1	2	4
Wesleyan Methodist, ..	500	6.000	—	—	—	—	—	1	1
New Jerusalem, ...	325	4.400	—	—	—	1	—	1	2
Jews Synagogue, ...	300	8.000	1	—	—	—	—	—	1
Moravian Church,......	—	—	1	—	—	—	—	—	1
Asso. Scotch Pres'terian,	300	3.000	—	—	—	—	—	1	1
Indian Church,........	150	200	—	1	—	—	—	—	1
Union Houses,........	491	3.500	1	—	—	—	2	—	3
	104.132	$1.526.200	44	47	11	32	58	48	240

Having examined the preceding schedule, I doubt not some will think that, if there be in the State 104,-132 seats for a population of 165,400, (making all requisite allowance for invalids and children,) there has been an equitable provision made for the inhabitants.—But it ought not to be forgotten that many of these houses are so situated, as to be of little advantage to the people, they not having been used for years. Besides, deducting the returns from the two cities, amounting to 61,000, there will remain for 104,400 persons, 60,916 seats. But there are neighborhoods, as you have seen that need immediate attention. I do not, however, dwell so much upon additional houses, as upon the necessity of improving the condition of our population and providing means for the education of the generations growing up among us. In respect to pew or seat accommodations, Rhode Island compares very favorably with her sister States in New England. There is a house for about every six hundred and ninety inhabitants. The difficulty more especially is, that the citizens do not attend public worship, a fault not peculiar to Rhode Island, for she is excelled in this respect by few. The average attendance of the people at large, does not probably exceed one in five. Rarely, it is believed, are there found on any ordinary Sabbath in Rhode Island, one fifth of the population assembled in religious bodies.— Such a number would fill one-third of every house, used and not used in the State; a spectacle that has never yet been witnessed.

As a denomination, we have failed in our duty in not causing the gospel to be preached in all our towns, as was required by the very Providence that made this a Baptist State. Nevertheless, I repeat, I rejoice, and will rejoice, that notwithstanding our inertness as a people, Christians of other denominations have come up to this work. But this does not release us from our obligation. Our interests that wilt in the sunshine, need to be resuscitated, and new standards to be set up. We require an increase of an able and judicious ministry.— We are suffering through lack of pastoral labor. Besides, we have virtually fifteen vacant pastorships, and five more will occur unless the churches are relieved from their pecuniary embarrassments. Some of these embarrassments are not only exceedingly oppressive, but there is great danger that after the pastors have resigned, the meeting-houses will pass into the hands of those who have no sympathy with the truth as we receive it. Our ministry is scantily supported, and on this account many leave the pastorship. There is unquestionably a fault in this matter in the ministry, as well as in the churches. In some sections, the people have been educated to believe that they commit a moral wrong in remunerating any one for his religious services, and some ministers have come to see, that in this respect, they themselves have greatly erred. It is time that we cease to say so much concerning a hireling ministry, and that both ministers and people, devote their means and energy to the dissemination of the truth. And if we desire to retain our children when educated, we must provide, under God, such a ministry of the word as can instruct them in the truth as it is in Jesus ;—a ministry that shall be educated so as to be able to explain our doctrines and enforce obedience to the glorious gospel of the blessed God. Not that I believe that every minister must of necessity receive a liberal education, desirable as this is in all ordinary circumstances. I would advocate, however, a ministry filled with the power and spirit of the Holy Ghost, without which, every degree of knowledge, useful as it becomes to every one called to the sacred office, profiteth not.

In this Colony, in 1738, there were less than 20,000 inhabitants, and thirty-three places of public worship, occupied by four religious denominations only; in 1853, the State contained 185,400 inhabitants and two hundred and fifty churches, constituting nearly twenty different religious orders of professing Christians.

I have prepared a table, which exhibits with a good deal of accuracy, the actual church membership at the present time in the State. And, as I am unable to complete the plan exhibited, it is proper that I should here state that, in relation to the Society of Friends, I have obtained the reports of their Monthly Meetings instituted in Rhode Island, and quote them as rendered to me, viz :—

" Rhode Island Monthly Meeting, 170 ; South Kingstown, do. 68 ; Greenwich, do. 133 ; Providence, do. 319 ; Smithfield, do. 233 ; and other members, 27—making a total of 950." In the city of Providence, there is a Mariner's Church of 50 members ; also, a Wesleyan Methodist, of 70 members ; a Scotch Presbyterian, of 143 members ; Colored Churches, as reported, of 200 members ; and of Second Adventists, numbering 200 communicants—in all, 1,640 members.

In relation to Roman Catholics, there are, as I learn, no communicants except such as go to the " Confessional" and receive on their confession and the promise to conform to the requisition of penance, permission from their priests " to communicate." Nor need we wonder how this can be performed, when it is known how many priests there are in Providence and other places. But the confessional !—an engine truly of great and fearful power, and objectionable, as it appears to me, because subversive alike of personal accountability and personal freedom, as well as of the Rhode Island doctrine of soul liberty.

And it is due to the principles which we as Baptists advocate, that I should here remark, that against the Romanists as a sect I have nothing here to say. Their right to believe in the articles of their church I do not question. They, as is true of all denominations, to their own Master must stand or fall. *In eternity both priest and people will give account to God the Judge of all.* But although I do not objcct to Romanists as a mere denomination, I do object to them and will protest against any man or set of men whether in the church or state, who say that there is no sin in taking a false oath before one denominated a "heretic," as many of the Romish clergy affirm, and who swear to support the constitution of the United States, when at the same time they are solemnly pledged to the dominion of the Pope at Rome. If any one prefers the Catholic faith, he is at liberty to do so, and should be protected in his right, as persons of other forms of worship are protected, by statute law; but no one has any moral right to take the oath of allegiance to the government of this country, while at the same time he is sworn to a church in a foreign land which is adverse to all our free institutions, not even excepting our munificent and excellent public schools, in which entire equality in every respect prevails. Indeed the rights of our citizenship should not be conferred upon any one who is not perfectly absolved from legal obligation to every other government; and this ought to be inserted in every oath administered at naturalization. While I say this in good faith, I would that it may ever be said of every American citizen, whenever occasion shall require, as was said of Roger Williams, that "he ever opposed, and that in print once and again, what he called the *bloody tenet*, i. e. every kind and degree of persecution for conscience sake. For cruel and impious it is to punish those who cannot change their opinions without light or reason, and will not dissemble against all reason and conscience." Give us Rhode-Island doctrine, this acorn of soil if it be, whose tree of oak will shoot forth branches and be clothed with foliage, spreading a shade that will yet turn the melting, burning rays of oppression from the heads of men who are born, and who ought to be, and who are, and who have a right to be free and independent, and who should be responsible alone for their religion to the Lord of the conscience.

CHURCH MEMBERSHIP IN RHODE-ISLAND, 1853.

TOWNS.	Associated Baptists.	Six Principle Baptists.	Episcopalians.	Orthordox Congregationalist.	Unitarian Congregationalist.	Methodist Episcopal.	Christians.	Free Will Baptists.	Seventh Day Baptists.	Universalists.	New Jerusalem.	Total communicants in each Town.	Year of settlement.
Providence,	1849	....	738	1426	365	931	270	386	....	123	25	6113	1636
Portsmouth,	....	....	39	....	....	50	55	....	....	....	....	144	1638
Newport,	781	....	457	150	40	222	....	60	28	....	....	1738	1639
Warwick,	483	67	30	43	....	167	....	57	....	....	15	862	1642
Westerly,	328	....	161	....	....	44	90	....	241	....	....	864	1669
New Shoreham,	231	....	....	....	....	....	....	148	....	....	....	379	1672
East Greenwich,	200	15	61	....	....	175	....	....	....	....	....	451	1677
Jamestown,	....	....	14	....	....	....	....	14	....	....	....	28	1678
North Kingston,	442	46	35	....	....	....	....	42	....	....	....	565	1722
South Kingston,	420	....	58	41	....	....	....	113	20	....	....	652	1722
Smithfield,	179	....	101	239	....	30	....	190	....	....	....	739	1730
Glocester,	....	....	25	18	....	....	....	116	....	....	....	159	1730
Scituate,	60	412	....	57	....	....	....	377	....	....	....	906	1730
Charlestown,	77	....	....	....	....	....	....	59	....	....	....	136	1738
West Greenwich,	129	56	....	....	....	....	....	59	....	....	....	244	1741
Coventry,	106	619	....	20	....	....	....	....	....	....	....	745	1741
Exeter,	190	44	....	....	....	....	....	....	....	....	....	234	1742
Middletown,	....	....	8	....	....	....	80	....	....	....	....	88	1743
Little Compton,	....	....	....	197	....	88	....	....	....	....	....	285	1746
Tiverton,	35	....	....	89	....	....	....	125	....	....	....	249	1746
Bristol,	117	....	285	248	....	292	125	....	....	....	....	1067	1746
Warren,	258	....	125	....	....	264	....	....	....	....	....	647	1746
Cumberland,	295	....	113	43	....	253	....	....	....	90	....	794	1746
Richmond,	80	460	....	....	....	....	....	....	....	....	....	540	1747
Cranston,	67	47	....	23	....	....	....	30	....	....	....	167	1754
Hopkinton,	324	....	....	....	....	22	....	....	766	....	....	1112	1757
Johnston,	....	....	22	....	....	....	....	357	....	....	....	379	1759
North Providence,	495	....	200	119	....	160	...	40	....	30	....	1044	1765
Barrington,	....	....	....	107	....	....	....	....	....	....	....	107	1770
Foster,	....	....	....	....	....	....	....	296	....	....	....	296	1781
Burrillville,	....	....	....	....	....	126	....	175	....	....	....	301	1806
31 Towns.	7146	1766	2472	2820	305	2824	620	2644	1055	243	40	22035	

There are connected with the several denominational churches, besides the Romanists, 23,650 members, of which number the Associated Baptists have 7146 ; and the whole number of communicants who practise the New Testament baptism is 13,231. There are therefore 9469 Pedobaptists,13,231 Baptists,and 1640 Friends and others, (see page 100) making the aggregate of 23,650 members. There may be 24,000 in the State who are professors of religion. Immersion is frequently performed by other denominations besides the Baptists.

I have endeavored to be accurate as possible in the number of churches, but in a few instances, by taking in the meeting-houses, I find I have exceeded their several reports, but this will not vary the denominational interests but little if any; for in some instances there are houses of worship in towns adjacent to those towns in which the churches are located, so that the denominational representations remain unchanged. But if there be any errors, the fault is in the returns of the census. There were in June 1850, 221 independent churches returned. In the various orders there have been since that time several new churches formed, which are included in this report.

The Associated Baptists have two Associations. The first is called, "The WARREN ASSOCIATION," which was formed in Warren, September 1767. Its Eighty-sixth anniversary was held in the Third Baptist Meeting-house in Providence August 31, 1853. The second is known by the name of "The PROVIDENCE BAPTIST ASSOCIATION ;" it was established at a meeting of delegates from several churches held in the Cumberland Hill Baptist Meeting-house, October 9th, 1843. The Tenth anniversary was observed in the Fourth Baptist Meeting-house in Providence, September 21st, 1853. These two associations also meet annually on the last Tuesday of April, as "The Rhode-Island Baptist State Convention." This Convention was constituted in Providence, August 4th, 1825. Its twenty-eighth anniversary was celebrated in the First Baptist Meeting-house in Providence, June 22d, 1853. Its Board of Managers meet quarterly on the last Tuesday in July, October, January and April.

"The Old Six Principle, or General Baptist Conference," met and celebrated its one hundred and eighty-third anniversary in the Knightville Meeting-house, Cranston, September 9th, 10th, 11th, 1853, having been formed in 1670. Its quarterly meetings are held on Saturday, before the first Sunday in November, and Saturday, before the second Sunday in April, and Saturday, before the third Sunday in July, and on Friday, before the second Sunday in September.

"The Free Will Baptist Connexion" hold their quarterly meetings on Wednesday, before the fourth Sabbath in January, May, August and October.

The Christian Denomination, have their regular meetings, but I have been unable to learn their arrangements.

"The Seventh-Day Baptist Eastern Association," meets annually in May. Its seventeenth anniversary was held in Piscataway, New Jersey, Thursday, May 26th, 1853. The Executive Committee meet on Wednesday, before the third Sabbath or Saturday in November, and on Thursday, before the fourth Sabbath or Saturday in May.

"The Sixty-Third Annual Convention of the Protestant Episcopal Church," was held in Grace Church, Providence, June 14th, 1853.

" THE FIFTIETH ANNUAL MEETING OF THE EVANGELICAL CONSOCIATION," was held in the Congregational Meeting house, in Barrington, June 14th, 1853—*Its Jubilee Anniversary.*

" THE PROVIDENCE ANNUAL CONFERENCE OF THE METHODIST EPISCOPAL CHURCH," was held in the Fourth Street Church, in New Bedford, (Mass.) April 13th, 1853 ; its thirteenth session.

" THE UNITARIAN AUTUMNAL CONVENTION," was held in Worcester, October 18th, 1853.

" THE NEW ENGLAND YEARLY MEETING OF THE SOCIETY OF FRIENDS," meets in Newport, on the first seventh, after the second sixth day in the sixth month, or on Saturday after the second Friday in June. Meetings for worship, are held the next day. This meeting was established earlier than in 1671, but how much before that year it is not known, as the records were consumed with a dwelling-house, in which they were kept. It is safe to record that its one hundred and eighty-third anniversary was held in Newport, June 11th, 1853. The Rhode Island Quarterly Meeting was established in 1699. This meeting embraces the five Monthly Meetings that exist in the State.

" THE UNIVERSALIST CONVENTION," meets on the third Wednesday in May.

The NEW JERUSALEM CHURCH in Rhode-Island have no united Covocation, nor any general meetings, so far as I can ascertain.

POPULATION AND VALUATION OF RHODE ISLAND, 1730–1854.

TOWNS.	Population in 1730.	Population in June, 1774.	Population in June, 1850.	Population in January, 1854.	Valuation. January, 1782.	Valuation in June, 1850.	Valuation in January, 1854.
NEWPORT CO.							
Newport,.........	4.640	9.209	9.563	11.000	$510.000	$4.880.450	$8.000.000
Portsmouth,......	813	1.512	1.833	2.000	183.333	1.114.950	1.500.000
Jamestown,......	321	563	358	400	66.666	282.100	300.000
Middletown,......	......	881	832	1.000	113.333	825.500	1.200.000
Tiverton,.........	......	1.957	4.699	5.000	368.333	1.926.140	2.000.000
Little Compton,...	......	1.232	1.462	1.600	297.666	985.605	1.000.000
New Shoreham,..	290	575	1.262	1.300	....	414.550	500.000
PROVIDENCE CO.							
Providence,.......	3.916	4.321	41.513	50.000	723.333	33.511.000	37.500.000
Smithfield,.......	......	2.888	11.500	12.000	666.666	5.040.250	5.100.000
Scituate,.........	......	3.601	4.582	5.000	356.666	1.811.150	1.900.000
Glocester,........	......	2.945	2.872	3.000	526.666	1.014.000	1.100.000
Cumberland,......	......	1.756	6.662	7.000	302.773	3.224.250	3.300.000
Cranston,.........	......	1.834	4.312	7.000	411.133	2.176.100	2.223.000
Johnston,.........	......	1.031	2.937	3.000	214.000	1.126.200	1.200.000
North Providence.	......	830	7.680	8.000	152.913	3.557.800	3.600.000
Foster,...........	......	......	1.932	2.000	253.333	576.340	577.000
Burrillville,.......	......	......	3.538	3.600	....	948.730	1.000.000
WASHINGTON CO.							
Westerly,.........	1.926	1.812	2.766	3.500	323.333	1.250.000	1.500.000
North Kingston,..	2.105	2.472	2.971	3.100	495.500	1.380.590	1.500.000
South Kingston,..	1.523	2.835	3.802	4.000	974.333	1.502.550	1.600.000
Charlestown,.....	......	1.821	994	1.000	274.000	322.312	322.000
Richmond,........	......	1.257	1.784	1.800	234.533	569.096	600.000
Hopkinton,........	......	1.805	2.478	2.500	303.333	685.700	700.000
Exeter,...........	......	1.864	1.635	1.700	342.900	584.940	600.000
BRISTOL CO.							
Bristol,...........	......	1.209	4.616	5.000	217.466	2.954.300	3.400.000
Warren,..........	......	979	3.103	3.300	130.000	1.639.300	2.000.000
Barrington,......	......	601	795	900	102.400	513.954	600.000
KENT CO.							
East Greenwich,..	1.223	1.663	2.358	2.500	265.333	763.995	800.000
West Greenwich,..	......	1.764	1.350	1.400	244.333	452.958	453.000
Warwick,.........	1.178	2.438	7.740	8.000	583.666	3.032.154	3.500.000
Coventry,........	......	2.023	3.620	3.800	333.333	1.753.150	1.800.000
	17.935	59.678	147.549	165.400	$9.968.277	$80.820.114	$91.375.000

RECAPITULATION.

Newport County,.	6.064	15.929	20.009	22.300	$1.539.331	$10.429.295	$14.500.000
Providence..“....	3.916	19.206	87.528	100.600	3.607.483	52.985.820	57.500.000
Washington.“....	5.554	13.866	16.430	17.600	2.944.932	6.295.188	6.822.000
Bristol......“....	......	2.789	8.514	9.200	449.866	5.107.554	6.000.000
Kent.........“....	2.401	7.888	15.068	15.700	1.426.665	6.002.257	6.553.000
Total Aggregate,	17.935	59.678	147.549	165.400	$9.968.277	$80.820.114	$91.375.000

SABBATH SCHOOLS.

The Sabbath School Department of our Churches meets annually in connection with the Rhode Island Baptist State Convention, on the Wednesday succeeding the fourth Tuesday in April, at 10 o'clock, A. M., and is known by the name of the SABBATH SCHOOL ASSOCIATION. It consists of delegates appointed by the several schools connected with the Convention. It elects its own officers, as specified in the seventh article of the constitution of the Convention, and occupies as much of the day as may seem from time to time necessary and desirable for the transaction of business pertaining to the Association. The next meeting will be opened by Asa Messer Gammell, the Chairman of a Committee of ten to whom the management of the Association is intrusted for the current year.

Of this department I shall at this time say but a word. In some of the churches there is manifestly great inefficiency; not even the children or the adults are gathered into the Sabbath School, and yet in the combinations of this world they enter or take an interest. But in most of our churches there are found collected groups of the old, the middle aged, and the young, who thus meet weekly for the purpose of receiving and imparting religious instruction.

I annex a Table which shows the condition of this field of our spiritual joys and hindrances.

SCHOOLS.	SUPERINTENDENTS.	Male Teachers.	Female Teachers.	Male Scholars.	Female Scholars.	Average of Teachers' attendance.	Average of Scholars' Attendance	Volumes in Library.	Aggregate of Teachers	Aggregate of Scholars.	Total Aggregate.
Prov. 1st, Church......	R. A. Guild, ...	14	24	109	145	34	182	400	38	254	292
" 2d,....."........	J. Boyce,........	7	8	97	103	12	133	320	15	200	215
" 3d,....."........	A. W. Godding,.	12	18	128	147	25	205	700	30	275	305
" 4th,..."........	S. R. Weeden,..	12	20	107	145	29	185	700	32	252	284
" 5th,..."........	J. S. Sibley,.....	3	7	25	30	8	40	150	10	55	65
" Meeting Street,...	G. C. Willis,....	4	6	20	25	9	33	300	10	45	55
" South,...........	J. C. Wightman,	5	9	65	75	11	130	450	14	140	154
" Eighth,..........	J. F. Jolls,......	6	6	40	70	12	90	450	12	110	122
" High Street,......	H. C. Marchant,	18	20	122	153	36	261	500	38	275	313
N. Prov. Allendale,...	S. Belden,.......	7	10	75	100	14	140	482	17	175	192
" Fruit Hill,........	B. A. Whipple, .	2	4	18	32	5	30	500	6	50	56
" 1st, Pawtucket...	S. G. Benedict,..	12	13	100	132	20	175	700	25	282	257
" High st. Pawt'ket	O. Keach,.......	6	9	50	59	10	75	250	15	109	124
Smithfield, Cent. Falls,	S. S. Mallery,...	10	10	85	115	18	150	500	20	200	220
" Lonsdale,........	M. Aldrich,.....	5	7	25	50	8	50	300	12	75	87
" L. R. & Albion,..	T. Mann,........	1	4	15	20	5	30	359	5	35	40
Cnmberland, Val. Falls	L. Flagg,........	4	6	45	55	8	75	400	10	100	110
Cumberland Hill,......	H. Sweet,.......	1	7	15	25	6	30	235	8	40	48
" Woonsocket,....	A. Ballou Jr....	6	9	71	81	8	100	300	15	152	167
Cranston, Pawtuxet,...	N. Lee,.........	3	15	40	53	14	70	300	18	93	111
Scituate, Fiskville.....	....	...	...	...	...	...	...	...	...	...	...
Warwick, Shawomet, .	G. A. Willard,..	...	8	20	30	6	33	200	8	50	58
" Natic,...........	S. R. Hopkins,,.	9	12	50	80	18	130	500	21	130	151
" Phœnix,........	J. A. Taylor,...	8	8	50	50	16	100	600	16	100	116
" First,............	P. Spencer,......	3	4	25	40	7	50	200	7	65	72
Coventry, Quidnic,....	H. Inman,......	5	7	40	60	11	65	405	12	100	112
" Central,..........	B. V. Gallup,...	10	10	75	75	18	80	600	20	150	170
East Greenwich,.......	A. Wall,........	5	8	30	60	10	75	200	13	90	103
West Greenwich,......	C. S. Hazard,....	3	1	15	15	4	30	150	4	30	34
N. Kingst. Quoitnesset,	J. L. Congdon,..	4	6	26	38	8	50	200	10	64	74
" First, Wickford,..	S. D. Reynolds,.	7	11	71	64	15	86	500	18	135	153
" First, N. K.......	J. Eldred,.......	5	4	34	16	8	36	450	9	50	59
Exeter Baptist Church,	G. Tillinghast,..	5	4	37	30	9	50	350	9	67	76
S. Kingston, First,....	J. P. Rodman,..	5	7	40	40	12	80	140	12	80	92
" Second,.........	E. H. Peckham,.	5	3	22	12	7	32	300	8	34	42
" Queen's River,...	J. W. Briggs,...	4	4	15	15	8	30	175	8	30	38
Richmond, 2d Church,	G. K. Clark,....	3	3	10	20	5	20	500	6	30	36
Hopkinton, Second,...	H. H. Richmond,	15	17	62	88	25	100	200	32	150	182
" First,............	....	...	...	...	...	...	...	...	...	...	...
Westerly, Niantic,.....	G. W. Champlain	9	3	10	10	4	15	175	12	20	32
" First,............	T. R. Hyde,.....	9	10	42	85	12	90	600	19	127	146
" Lottery Village,..	L. Hall.........	...	...	...	...	...	...	100	...	...	...
" Charlestown First	J. P. Burbank,..	1	2	25	30	2	45	50	3	55	58
New Shoreham,........	A. C. Rose,.....	8	5	36	54	7	60	200	13	90	103
Newport, First,.......	S. Albro,.......	6	16	70	80	14	75	400	22	150	172
" Second,.........	B. H. Rhoades,.	7	11	50	70	16	90	350	18	120	138
" Central,..........	W. C. Langley,.	13	31	125	160	36	200	838	44	285	329
Tiverton, Central,.....	A. Gray,.......	3	5	31	46	8	55	200	8	77	85
Bristol, First,.........	N. B. Cook,.....	5	7	50	40	10	70	375	12	90	102
Warren, First,........	A. M. Gammell,.	10	26	100	160	28	200	600	36	260	296
		305	445	2413	3083	616	4131	17854	750	5496	6246

From these statistics as now presented, it will be seen that we have forty-seven Sabbath Schools in this State, in which there are 750 teachers and 5496 scholars; of the teachers 305 are males, and 445 females; of the scholars 2413 are males, and 3083 females; the average attendance of teachers is 616, and of scholars 4131. Almost every church has a Library for its Sabbath School, whether at present closed or open, the whole number of volumes amounting, as nearly as I can ascertain, to 17,854. The whole number of scholars connected with the schools is 6,246.

Sabbath Schools likewise engage the sympathies and hearty cooperation of other denominations besides our own. The Congregationalists report 295 teachers and 2831 scholars; the Episcopalians 276 teachers and 2188 scholars; the Methodists about 300 teachers and 3000 scholars; besides schools of other denominations not here mentioned. The whole must amount to not less than 17,000 scholars, and 2,000 teachers. I have not seen any returns from other schools in the State, but make the above computations from facts that have been presented. It is greatly to be desired that this institution should receive the hearty cooperation and support of all our churches.

Admonished by the great remissness of our Denomination in our religious interests in the State, and encouraged by the mercy of Him who has neither abandoned us, nor as yet removed our candlesticks, but has granted us many tokens of promise, we should inquire, what He will have us do? And aware of what we *can* do, let us strengthen the things that languish and are ready to die. And what shall we do to meet our high responsibilities in a land where Baptist sentiments have always been so prevalent?

The fault is not to be ascribed, as some have claimed, to the laxity of our denominational tenets, nor to the weakness of the voluntary principle in our civil government. For our churches and our ministry can live without civil taxation, or government patronage. And this is apparent not in our own churches only, but in those of other sects; also by the conviction silently and constantly obtaining on this subject that no one in christian matters ought to be interrupted, or compelled; and that to the people in their voluntary associations should be committed the sustaining of their religious interests, as they in their wisdom and freedom, deem proper to provide. Our comparative weakness and inefficiency is not therefore to be traced to our political condition, but to our moral inertness.

And shall this inactivity and feebleness in our religious affairs continue? Shall this benumbing influence continue to blight our vines, and shall our fruit continue to blast, wither, and perish! In 1738 there were in the then nine towns on the main land eight Baptist churches, one in each town, save Greenwich. In this town, however, there was a Baptist meeting-house sometime previous to 1738, but this house, together with nearly all the meeting-houses of that time, are either removed or greatly dilapidated. And not only have the houses decayed, but the churches have waned, so that, aside from the first church in Providence, and some three others, there is now but a feeble trace of the existence of these early churches. When another century shall close, God forbid such a record of the churches now represented in this Convention.

On account of the fluctuating character of the factory population and of the introduction of foreign help, churches in one year represented as thriving, frequently in the lapse of a few years, become most essentially weakened by the loss of their members. And it is on this account that the Board of Managers have been unable to establish a standard for determining the amount of appropriations ; my own judgment is in favor of some uniform decreasing ratio, departures from which to be justified by the circumstances of the churches at the time of their application. And our true policy is to promote the liberal support of our pastors by every means within our power. Let us not muzzle the mouth that treadeth out the corn—surely not the mouth of them who bring us the word of the Lord.

From the returns now submitted to me in your name, and presented to you in this report, I regret to find that so little attention is given in the churches to benevolent contributions, prayer meetings for missions, Sabbath schools, to the seamen's cause, and to revivals ; and I regret also to find, that there exists so small a number of maternal meetings, and female prayer meetings—yet, it is interesting to observe, that religion is, by universal consent, the one thing, and the only thing that can really make a people happy. Would that such a vital interest might be felt in our Zion, by all our members, as would draw forth from every one of them the declaration of a deeply settled purpose, "Because of the house of the Lord our God, I will seek thy good."

As the Associated Baptists of Rhode Island, we have met in this Convention to consider by what means we may sow to better advantage the good seed of the word of God in the soil of our fathers, and bring to greater maturity that which was sown by them. And it is our privilege, and equally our obligation, to do what our hands find to do.

There are two kinds of work necessary to be done. The first relates to churches in a state of debility and in perplexing circumstances, into which they are not unfrequently cast. The second embraces the establishment of new interests, or the cultivation of the fields already opened and constantly being opened, inviting our toils, our prayers, and our sympathies. We have much to do, if we would improve the soil, or even prevent tares from being sown by the enemy, or check their growth when they have sprung up. Worse evils exist in our midst than existed thirty years ago, when generations died ignorant or but partially enlightened. Our towns are filling up with foreigners who know no religion but that which subverts the freedom secured to us by the Charter of Charles II, and provided for in our constitution. And not unfrequently our own citizens are found to sympathize with these foreigners. Efforts to subvert our freedom, bold and daring, are talked of openly. And unless we make strenuous efforts to secure a general moral culture and the preservation of our rights, we shall arrive at a condition in which there is no remedy without acting again the scenes of our ancestral reformers. Even in my day I have listened to expressions like these with slight emotion. I well remember when the lamented Going returned from his first western tour, and subsequently in his annual visits to New England, how earnestly he expressed his feelings, and with what pathos he dwelt on themes like these. But we heard him as a professional secretary. I have beheld fulfilled many of his sayings. And even in Rhode Island where were embodied first the conceptions of a charter of distinct civil and religious rights, I have seen the evidences of real danger. And with me you also perceive that but one step remains to be taken, in order that our very constitution become the vehicle to bring upon us all the evils which our forefathers dreaded, and from which they fled to this soil, as an asylum and a home. And I confess that to me it seems less strange than ever before, that as this State was the first public field of entire but separate civil and religious freedom, so it may be that the first altar upon which its adherents may be immolated to oppression in our day, shall here be erected.

The plan upon which I propose we should operate is, either, *first*, through some individual, duly appointed by you, whose duty it shall be, with the advice and under the direction of the Board, to nurse our feeble churches, and to preach as opportunities are presented the gospel in the State, seeking new situations and rearing new interests in our various counties; or, *second*, to divide the State into several districts, and after the plan of the Methodists in Wales, to appoint some minister, living in the district to which he may be designated, as the chairman of a committee, selected also from the same district, to whom the division shall be entrusted, with instructions to hold religious meetings in neighborhoods not fully occupied, and to visit the churches within their boundaries, and report to the Board, and through the Board to the Convention, at its annual sessions.

My own judgment favors the first arrangement; for, as every pastor has, or ought to have, all he can do in his own immediate neighborhood, I fear that there will be little efficiency, if we commit this work to separate committees. And so shall we all think, in my opinion, if there exist in the denomination the spirit of confidence and good feeling, so that they can intrust this high duty to a single person, whose mind shall be given wholly to the moral culture of the people;—who shall pursue no other than a christian and dignified service;—a service not of dollars mainly, but a pastoral, advisory, and ministerial service; a service involving whatsoever is true, honest, just, pure, lovely, and of good report;—whatsoever is praiseworthy in itself, or due to the ministry of Christ, performed by any ways or means which the great Head of the church shall indicate and approve as effectual in disseminating the principles of the new-testament, such as we believe all true Baptists profess, good, sound, and just principles; in a word, one who shall preach the word, hold religious meetings as he may be able; gather the Sabbath Schools together at different times in the year, embracing sections contiguous, and devote his entire energy to the cause of Christ in connection with our churches, not as a secular, but as a truly religious man; this I think will be doing the work with effective power, and filling a station, than which, none can be more honorable or more useful;—nor can there be any one human agency from which we can hope to reap so much advantage, if the Spirit attend the work, as He did in the times of the primative preachers, and as it is promised that He will accompany the faithful ministrations of the gospel.

In my late visits to our churches I have not gone as an agent, but as a minister of Christ. My business was not to obtain their pecuniary means, but to preach the gospel, to tender to them your christian salutation, endeavoring to stir up their minds to their obligations to Jesus Christ. I doubt not, however, should your suffrages be given, that he who accepts them, will put the people in a remembrance of their obligation, and at times even make direct application for funds to sustain the objects approved by you. But my impression is that Rhode Island needs, and imperiously demands, AN INFLUENCE EMINENTLY PASTORAL. For the want of it, she sadly bleeds; and in the absence of it, year after year, during our two centuries of civil existence, she has remained torpid; dying, yet breathing; yea, panting for that, she knew not what,—*this very pastoral power.* And as one among you, should such an appointment be made as I have described, I desire *that he may not be recognized, or spoken of as an Agent*, respectable and useful as such officers are in our many associations, *but as a minister among our churches, whose great duty it is, to improve to his utmost effort, under Christ*, OUR RHODE ISLAND BAPTIST STATE PASTORATE.

And in this place permit me to express my conviction that the proposition now presented, is practicable, and to assure you that the sympathies of the people to a very great extent will be with you in this measure. I have conversed with brethren in various towns, whose judgment approves it. And I see not why we should not immediately go forth into a territory, settled, and in the beginning for many years occupied almost exclusively by Baptists. Not that we would interfere with other forms of doctrine varying from our own, but on grounds sacred to all, act as those who are fully persuaded in their own minds, being accountable to no other than the Lord of the conscience for our religious belief, and in our actions also amenable only to him, unless we violate common law and offend against the civil rights of our neighbors; rights which law must protect, and which law, every member in the community ought by every means in his power fully to sustain, or suffer a righteous penalty.

In conclusion, tendering to you, my best wishes for your personal and mutual usefulness, I ask you to accept the printed and written report, made by each of our fifty-one churches, detailing vaiious facts connected with their respective bodies, and which I herewith lay on your table, to be placed upon the files of your secretary. Also, as much of the time of the Pastor of the Central Baptist Church in Newport, has been devoted to this mission, to an account of which you have now listened, I request your acceptance as from them of the bill of his travelling, postage, and other expenses, amounting in even figures, to seventy dollars.

And may the grace of the Lord Jesus Christ, and the love of God, and the communion of the Holy Ghost, be with you all.

Your servant for Jesus' sake,

HENRY JACKSON.

OFFICERS OF THE RHODE-ISLAND BAPTIST STATE CONVENTION FOR THE YEAR 1853-4.

President, JAMES N. GRANGER, Providence.
Vice-President, HENRY JACKSON, Newport.
Corresponding Secretary, ————
Recording Secretary, JOSEPH C. HARTSHORN, Providence.
Treasurer, RHODES B. CHAPMAN, Providence.

BOARD OF MANAGERS.

F. Wayland, Providence,
T. C. Jameson, "
B. Spencer, Lippitt and Phenix,
F. Smith, Providence,
S. W. Field, Providence,
James Boyce, "
B. Peck, "
S. Adlam, Newport,
J. O. Choules, "
B. Miner, Providence,
A. M. Gammell, Warren,
F. Denison, Westerly,
Wm. Phillips, Providence,
George Pierce, Pawtuxet,
J. H. Read, Providence,
J. B. Breed, Woonsocket,
J. E. Chesshire, Wickford,
E. Savage, Pawtucket,
V. J. Bates, Providence,
J. C. Welsh, "
I. M. Church, S. Kingston.

AUDITORS.

Asa Newell, Providence,
J. H. Read, Providence.

LIFE-MEMBERS OF THE CONVENTION, 1854.

Adlam Rev. Samuel,
Albro Stephen B.
*Allen John,
Amsbury Jesse,
Andrews William,
Anthony Lorenzo D.
Arnold Rev. Albert N.
Arnold Mrs. Frances R.
Arnold Richard J.
Asher Rev. Jeremiah,
Avery William D.
Aylesworth John,
Babcock Amos,
Babcock Cyril,
Bailey Benjamin D.
Bailey Mrs. Urania L.
Baker Elisha W.
Baker Rev. John H.
Barker Simeon,
Barker Wm. H.
Barrows E. S.
Barrus William L.
Bates Mrs. Joanna,
Bates Nahum,
Bates Varnum J.
*Bates Whitman,
Benedict Rev. D.
Benedict S. Gano,
Benedict Uriah,
Bishop Nathan,
Blake David B.
Boise Prof. James R.
Boardman George D.
Bowen Allan, jun.
Boyce James,
Bradford Rev. S. S.
Bradley William,
Brayton Rev. Jonathan,
Brown Rev. Allen,
Brown Hugh H.
Budlong James E.
Budlong Rebecca A.
Buffington George W.
Bullock Mrs. Anna D.
Bump Nathaniel,
Burdick Rev. D. M.
Burgess Alexander,
Burgess Rev. I. J.
Burrows John R.
Rutler James H.
Byram Rev. B. P.
Cannon John,
Carr Mrs. Mary T.
Carr T. T.
Caswell Rev. Alexis,
Chace Prof. George I.
Chace Otis,
Chace Perry J.
Chaplin Rev. Jeremiah
Chapman Rhodes B.
Chesshire Rev. J. E.
Choules Rev. John O.
Clapp Russell,
Clark Rev. George K.
Clark Mrs. Lydia,
Cogswell Rev. Wilson,
Cole Samuel J.
Coleman Jesse,
Crandall Henrie,
Crocker Rev. G. D.
Crooker Josiah F.
Daniels Dexter,
*Daniels George P.
Daniels Hannah P.
Davis Rev. John,

*Deceased.

Day Daniel,
Dayton L.
Denham Daniel C.
Denison Rev. F.
*Dexter John,
*Dexter Levi C.
Dexter Mrs. Sarah,
Douglas Rev. William
Dowling Rev. John,
Dowling Rev. Thomas,
Drowne Henry B.
Driscoll Hannah,
Durfee Sanford,
Eddy Richard E.
Eddy John S.
Elliott Lemuel H.
*Ellis Augustus,
Ely Dr. J. W. C.
Fairbrother Lewis,
*Fenner Thomas,
Field Rev. Samuel W.
Foley Thomas W.
Fuller Rev. Edward K.
Fyfe Rev. Robert A.
Fyfe Mrs. Rebecca S.
Gammell A. M.
Gammell Prof. Wm.
Gamwell Albert A.
Gerald Samuel A.
Giles Miss Susan H.
Goddard Isaac,
Goff Ira D.
Gorham Charles,
Gowdey James A.
Gower Rev. H. B.
Graves Rev. J. M.
Granger Rev. J. N.
Green Mrs. Cornelia E.
Green Russell,
Greene Benjamin,
Greene John W.
Greene Prof. S. S.
Green William C.
Greenwood Walter,
Guild George,
Guild Reuben A.
Hague Rev. William,
Hail George,
Ham William,
Harkness Albert,
Hazard Joseph W.
Hedden Rev. B. F.
Hoar Lewis,
Holroyd James M.
Holyrod Mrs. C. V.
Howland Benj. B.
Hudson William H.
Humphreys Wm. S.
Ives Mrs. Hope,
Jackson Rev. Henry,
Jackson Mrs. Maria T.
Jackson Phebe,
Jameson Rev. T. C.
Jameson Mrs. Lucinda L.
Jastram George B.
Jenckes Jabez W.
Jencks J. F.
Jolls John F.
Kingsley James W.
Knowles Mrs. Susan E.
Lake William D.
Langley Joshua H.
Langley Nath'l H.
Langley William C.
Lawton Gideon,
Lincoln Rev. J. W.
Lincoln Prof. John L.
Ludlow Clarissa Ann,
Ludlow Sally L
Luther Job,
Lyon Merrick,
Manchester Giles,
Marchant Henry,
Marsh Benjamin,
Martin Philip W.
Martin Silvanus G.
Mason George B.
Mason Joseph R.
Mason Nathan
Mason Stephen G.
Mathewson Mrs. E.
Mathewson Nathan F.
Matteson Rev. N. H.
Millard William C.
Miller Mrs. Ann Eliza,
Miller Frederick,
*Miller Pardon,
Miner Rev. Bradley,
Morse Susan,
Munger Enos,
Newell Asa,
Northup Thomas G.
Olney James,
Paine John J.
Pattison Rev. R. E.
Pearce Mrs. Lydia,
Peck George B.
Peck George H.
Peck Josias L.
Philips Rev. William,
Pierce Rev. George,
Pike Jonathan,
Potter Miss Maria L.
Prevaux Rev. Francis E.
Read Cyrus B.
Read James H.
Read Joshua,
Rhodes Benjamin H.
Rhodes Rev. Christ'r.
Richards Rev. Samuel,
Richardson T. A.
Rogers Mrs. Eliza R.
Rogers Zoan,
Ross Daniel V.
Rounds Daniel,
Robbins Charles,
Russell Rev. J. W.
Salisbury Luther,
Sanders Edwin,
Satterlee A. B.
Saunders Henry,
Saunders Jacob,
Savage Rev. Edward,
Schubarth N. B.
Seabury T. M.
Seagraves Rev. E.
Serrington Rev. W. B.
*Shaw Charles,
Shaw George C.
Sheldon Miss Mary,
Sherman George J.
Sherman James H.
Slater Mrs. Sarah J.
Slocum S.
Slocum Samuel D.
Smith Edward,
Smith Rev. Francis,
Smith Rev. Joseph,
Spencer Wm. B.
Spink Nicholas N.
Stevens Philip,
Stewart Rev. Henry G.
Stillman Ira,
Stillman O. M.
Stillwell Abraham G.
Stillwell Samuel S.
Stone Gilman,
Stuart A. P. S.
Sweet Menzies,
Taylor Rev. A. H.
Teft Thomas A.
*Thayer Seth,

Thurber Miss Hetty,	Waterman George,	*Whipple Arnold,
Tillinghast Allen,	Wayland Rev. Francis,	Whipple Mrs. Phebe,
Tillinghast Charles E.	Wayland Heman L.	White Franklin,
Tillinghast Rev. J. A.	Wayland Mrs. H. S. H.	Wilbur Asa,
Tobey Rev. Zalmon,	Wells Elisha C.	Willard Rev. Geo. A.
Townsend Solomon,	Welch Stillman,	Willard Lucius A.
Verrinder Rev. Wm.	Welsh Rev. John C.	Willis George C.
Vincent Joseph R.	Wheaton James,	Woods Rev. Alva,
Wadsworth J. A.	Wheeler O. C.	Yeomans Henry P.
Wait Gideon,	Whipple Miss Anna,	Yorke John,
Warren David B.		

[Life members whose names are omitted in the above list, will please mention the fact to the Recording Secretary.]

The following named persons sustain the office of the Christian Ministry in Rhode Island, according to the usages of their respective denominational orders. The names of those not pastors are in italics.

• Associated Baptists.—*Francis Wayland*, James N. Granger, *Alexis Caswell*, *Alva Woods*, *William Douglass*, *Henry Day*, Samuel W. Field, *John C. Welsh*, *William Philips*, *J. C. Hartshorn*, Bradley Miner, Chauncey G. Leonard, Warren Randolph, George R. Darrow, *Perry Davis*, *Francis Smith*, *William B. Serrington*, *Zalmon Tobey*, John O. Choules, Edward Savage, Jonathan Brayton, David M. Burdick, Isaac N. Hobart, George Pierce, *J. F. Bigelow*, ——— Warren, John E. Chesshire, C. Casson Lewis, Samuel Adlam, George H. Clark, Benedict Johnson, Jun., Isaac M. Church, F. Denison, J. A. Tillinghast, John Tillinghast, S. A. Thomas, Benjamin F. Hedden, S. B. Bailey, J. P. Burbank, G. A. Willard, Henry Jackson, Ira Bates, J. W. Allen, A. A. Ross, A. Sheldon, G. Silver, *D. Benedict*, J. B. Breed, F. Wiley, J. Blain, *S. S. Mallery*, *S. S. Bradford*, *E. Seagraves*, *P. Tillinghast*, ——— Palmer, *W. Archer*, *R. Dennis*, E. J. Lock. Pastors supplying regularly 38—others 20—in all 58.

Six Principle Baptists.—John Gardner, John Slocum, Thomas Tillinghast, S. Kenyon, T. S. Tillinghast, J. Tillinghast, D. R. Knight, *J. Potter*, W. P. Place, *P. Harrington*, *W. Pearce*, *G. W. Potter*, *S Knight*, *A. Aldrich*, W. R. Slocum, *D. Slocum*, *B. B. Cottrel*, *N. W. Warner*, *A. J. Harrington*, *W. Storier*, *S. Matteson*, *R. Knight.*

Free Will Baptists.—G. T. Day, E. Scott. *J. Pratt*, E. R. Rose, W. H. Hastings, R. Allen, *H. Quimby*, *A. Brown*, J. B. Smith, *P. Nocake*, E. Noyes, D. Lancaster, M. Phillips, *J. S. Mowry*, J. A. M'Kenzie, B. Phalon, D. P. Harrison, *A. Durfee*, *E. White*, D. Williams, H. C. Hopkins, *T. C. Brown*, *W. N. Patt*, L. Parker, W. Dick, D. Carr, J. Hammond, D. R. Whittemore, E. R. Littlefield.

Christian Baptists.—A. G. Martin, D. Knowlton, J. Onell, W. Shurtleff, C. Bugbee, G. L. Smith, J. Wallen, J. Burlingame, M. B. Hopkins, N. Luther, J. Taylor, *N. Sweet*, *G. Williams.*

Seventh Day Baptists.—L. Crandall, C. Lewis, D. Coon, H. Clark, J. Greene, A. B. Burdick.

Episcopalians.—N. B. Crocker, G. Taft, H. Waterman, J. Trapnell, Jun., J. Kellog, D. C. Millett, H. Williams, D. R. Brewer, B. Watson, K. J. Stewart, T. H. Vail, B. P. Talbot, G. W. Hathaway, E. P. Gray, S. A. Crane, F. J. Warner, W. H. Mills, G. W. Chevers, E. F. Watson, G. Anthony, J. H. Eames, *J. Bristed*, *L. Burge*, *J. H. Carpenter*, *R. B. Fairbain*, *D. Henshaw*, *E. L. Drown*, *E. W. Stokes*, *P. Tocque.*

Congregationalists, Orthodox.—S. S. Hyde, T. Shepard, S. Blane, D. Andrews, J. Leavitt, T. A. Taylor, J. Mann, C. C. Beaman, S. Wolcott, R. H. Conklin, O.

F. Otis, G. Uhler, J. C. Seagrave, R. Toney, L. Swain, T. Thayer, E. H. Blanchard, J. Reid, *S. S. Tappan.*

Associate Presbyterian.—*A. H. Dumont, R. P. Dunn,* (*O. S.*)

Congregationalists, Unitarian.—E. B. Hall, C. T. Brooks, F. H. Hedge, E. M. Stone.

Wesleyan Methodist—J. M. H. Dow.

Methodist Episcopal.—S. C. Brown, D. Patten, J. Hinson, W. T. Harlow, J. Cady, S. Benton, G. W. Stearns, J. Lovejoy, C. Hammond, C. Banning, C. Nason, P. Crandon, H. H. Smith, E. A. Lyon, W. Cone, C. S. Hazard, H. C. Atwater, B. Allyn, L. B. Bates, *D. Fillmore, J. Fillmore,* E. S. Stanley, G. C. Bancroft.

Universalists.—E. A. Eaton, T. D. Cook, B. B. Nicholas, A. C. Abbot, J. Boyden, Jun.

Swedenborgians.—J. Prentice, —— Greene.

Second Advent.—G. W. Burnham, G. Needham.

Roman Catholics.—B. O'Reiley, J. Hughes, O. Gorman, J. Stokes, T. Quinn, D. Wheeler, P. Delancy, P. Lanaham, J. O'Reilly, J. Gibson, J. Fitten, J. McName, J. P. Cahill, P. Lamb, H. Carmody.

Society of Friends.—T. Anthony, R. Greene, E. Peckham, T. C. Collins, L. Almy, S. B. Tobey, J. Meader, E. Meader, H. Meader, H. Robinson, A. D. Wing, M. Beede, T. Gould, G. Congdon.

Great interest has been recently created among all denominations of christians in the cause of ministerial education, because of the great want of ministers to preach the word of life. In the records of the last Providence Annual Conference of the Methodist Episcopal Church, the following resolution, expressive alike of the feelings of every christian heart, was unanimously adopted; it exhibits the convictions of that body of believers on this subject.

"*Resolved*, In view of the great want of ministers to supply the work within the bounds of this Conference, that the first Friday in September be observed as a day of Fasting and Prayer, and that on said day our people be respectfully requested to assemble in their places of worship, and humbly, unitedly, and earnestly implore 'the Lord of the harvest to send forth more laborers into His harvest,' and that the Baptism of the Holy Ghost may be graciously vouchsafed to the Zion of God."

There are three principles laid down in a work published in 1681, which as Baptists, we shall, I trust, ever maintain and advocate, viz: "Taking the Holy Scriptures as their only perfect rule in all religious matters—allowing each rational person to judge of their meaning for himself—and holding that all the power of office and government in the church of Christ is derived from him, by his word and Spirit, to each particular church, and not by a local succession from any other power in the world." "And so far as any have declined from this last principle," the same writer remarks, "therein they have rejected a main reason of separation from the church of Rome."

To the reader, unacquainted with the facts, it may appear somewhat peculiar that so much has been printed in this volume respecting the senior Baptist date in this country. But as an *historical fact*, I felt that it was important that it should be determined; and also to account for the well known proceedings at the baptism of Williams. It appeared very strange, if, as has been claimed, Mr. Clark was a settled Baptist minister in Newport in March, 1638, that Mr. Williams and his ten associates, did not invite him to perform this sacred rite, instead of one of their own number; and especially as Mr. Williams and Mr. Clark, during their whole acquaintance, cherished towards each other the very kindest affection. The truth is, as I believe, Mr. Clark was not at that time an administrator. It is self evident if he had been, that Mr. Williams and his brethren would have availed themselves of his services. But I have as yet been unable from any source, to learn when Mr. Clark became a baptist, although he conducted religious meetings from 1638. Neither Comer nor Callender, say a word about it. If he was a baptist in England, he is not recognized as such in any journal now extant in this country before the schism in Newport in 1641, if indeed he was, according to Comer, (the earliest Baptist Historian in America) prior to 1644.

It is clear from Mr. Comer's manuscript, referred to on page 95, that in his opinion no church of any denomination had been formed on the Island prior to 1644, for in his History there named, he expressly states, that Mr. Clark and his friends, having secured a *civil* organization, *six years after their purchase*, sought to make provision for their souls through the establishment of a church, which they then (1644) formed.

It is to present Mr. Williams as the father of civil and religious liberty, and to identify the first christian baptism in America; to illustrate also the high position of Mr. Clark in the same respects for which Mr. Williams is distinguished, that the writer has entered upon this discussion.

Some few typographical errors have occurred, notwithstanding all the care that has been exercised. But

I am happy to state that these are merely such, except in the date of Washington County on page 35, which should be not 1779, but 1729; and on page 39, it should be John and Sarah Stanton; and the name Howes in the Warren church should be L. I. Hoar, and in the Lime Rock church, the deacon's name should be E. Ide; and in page 56, line 13th from the bottom, it should read "*are punished;*" and on page 68, the date should be not 1703, but 1803; and on page 77, the presiding officer of the Trustees, should be styled not President, but CHANCELLOR; and on page 94, the Clerk of the First Westerly Church should be Buel, and not Bull; and on page 95, the settlement of Rev. Mr. Granger should be 1842, and not 1853.

It is due also that I tender to REUBEN A. GUILD, Esq., of Providence, the thanks of the Board of the Convention for his exceedingly valuable services in the superintendance of this publication—a work of great care and patience. Also to Rev. Messrs. Burbank, Denison, and Brayton, and to Messrs. Steadman, Spencer, and Arnold of Cumberland, for their very kind and generous services in my tours. In relation to the city of Newport as described on page 29, the writer was led into a slight error. The true record is, having obtained a charter, the citizens accepted it June 1, 1784, and Hon. George Hazard was elected mayor, and P. Baker, clerk. This government continued until March 22, 1787, when by a political influence, created through the opposition of Mr. N. Easton to the decree of a mutual referee, by which the control of the first Beach had been awarded to the city, the charter was surrendered in conformity to the decision of the Legislature, and a vote of thanks passed on the 27th, to the city officers for the efficient and excellent services they had performed; who were also, as additional testimony of the public confidence, elected to the Town Council immediately upon the return of the city to its original town government. But Mr. Easton in the end secured nothing hereby; for the Beach, from the period of that decision has been, as at present it is, under the government of the constituted authorities of Newport.

CIVIL GOVERNMENT OF RHODE ISLAND,

JANUARY, 1854.

FRANCIS M. DIMOND, BRISTOL,
GOVERNOR AND EX-OFFICIO PRESIDENT OF THE SENATE;
——— LIEUTENANT GOVERNOR.

ASA POTTER of South Kingstown, *Secretary of State.*
WALTER S. BURGES of Cranston, *Attorney General.*
EDWIN WILBUR of Newport, *General Treasurer.*
LUCIAS C. ASHLEY, *Clerk of the Senate.*
BENJ. F. THURSTON, *Speaker of the House.*
WILLIAM J. MILLER and JOHN EDDY, *Clerks of the House.*

SENATORS AND REPRESENTATIVES.

TOWNS. NEWPORT. *Senator*—Isaac P. Hazard. *Representatives*—Henry Y. Cranston, Joseph Anthony, Thomas R. Hunter, Seth Bateman, John T. Bush.

MIDDLETOWN. *Senator*—John Gould. *Representative*—Abner Ward.

PORTSMOUUH. *Senator*—George W. Chace. *Representative*—George Manchester.

TIVERTON. *Senator*—Joseph Osborne. *Representatives*—George W. Humphrey, Augustus Chace, Nathaniel B. Durfee.

LITTLE COMPTON. *Senator*—Nathaniel Church. *Representative*—Oliver C. Brownell.

NEW SHOREHAM. *Senator*—Samuel Dunn. *Representative*—Anderson C. Rose.

JAMESTOWN. *Senator*—George C. Carr. *Representative*—William A. Weeden, Jun.

PROVIDENCE. *Senator*—Thomas P. Shepard. *Representatives*—Edward S. Lyon, Henry J. Angell, Americus V. Potter, Samuel True, Clarke Steere, Henry J. Burroughs, Nathaniel A. Eddy, Daniel Remington, Benjamin F. Thurston, William E. Peck, Benjamin B. Knight, Thomas Pierce, Jr.

SMITHFIELD. *Senator*—Robert Harris. *Representatives*—Israel Sayles, John Fenner, Emor Coe, Thomas Steere, Elisha Mowry, 2d, Samuel D. Slocum.

GLOCESTER. *Senator*—Cyrus Farnum. *Representatives*—Jesse P. Ballou, George L. Owen.

SCITUATE. *Senator*—Ira Cowee. *Representatives*—Jonah Titus, Albert K. Barnes.

CRANSTON. *Senator*—H. A. Potter. *Representatives*—Almoran Harris, Albert S. Gallup.

JOHNSTON. *Senator*—Alfred Anthony. *Representatives*—William Baker, William H. Matthewson.

NORTH PROVIDENCE. *Senator*—Charles S. Bradley. *Representatives*—John Tucker, William E. Dodge, Enoch Brown, John H. Weeden.

CUMBERLAND. *Senator*—Lyman Burlingame. *Representatives*—Lewis B. Arnold, John E. Brown, Mowry Taft, William Whipple.

BURRILVILLE. *Senator*—Burrill Logee. *Representatives*—Esten Angell Josiah S. Thayer.

FOSTER. *Senator*—William G. Stone. *Representative*—Richard Howard.

NORTH KINGSTON. *Senator*—John J. Reynolds. *Representatives*—Sylvester G. Shearman, George A. Davis.

SOUTH KINGSTON. *Senator*—Stephen A. Wright. *Representatives*—John C. Perry, George L. Hazard.

WESTERLY. *Senator*—Charles Maxon. *Representative*—Nathan F. Dixon.

CHARLESTOWN. *Senator*—Jos. H. Cross. *Representative*—Joseph Gavitt.

RICHMOND. *Senator*—George Weeden. *Representative*—Daniel Kenyon.

HOPKINTON. *Senator*—John S. Champlin. *Representative*—Jonathan R. Wells.

EXETER. *Senator*—Isaac Greene. *Representative*—John Hoxie.

WARWICK. *Senator*—John Brown Francis. *Representatives*—Simon H. Greene, Christopher Holden, Pardon Spencer, Randall Holden, 2d.

COVENTRY. *Senator*—William S. Harris. *Representatives*—Cromwell Whipple, Levi Johnson.

EAST GREENWICH. *Senator*—Walter Spencer. *Representative*—John Shippee.

WEST GREENWICH. *Senator*—Thomas T. Hazard. *Representative*—William B. Whitford.

BRISTOL. *Senator*—Benjamin Hall. *Representatives*—John B. Munro, J. Russell Bullock.

WARREN. *Senator*—Henry H. Luther. *Representatives*—Alfred Bosworth, Rodolphus B. Johnson.

BARRINGTON. *Senator*—Allin Bicknell. *Representative*—Pardon Clarke.

SUPREME COURT OF RHODE ISLAND.

RICHARD W. GREENE of Providence, *Chief Justice.*

LEVI HAILE of Warren, *Associate Justice.*

WILLIAM R. STAPLES of Providence, *Associate Justice.*

GEORGE A. BRAYTON of Warwick, *Associate Justice.*

	CLERKS OF SUPREME COURT.	CLERKS OF COURT COM. PLEAS.
Newport County,	George C. Shaw,	George C. Shaw,
Providence "	Edwin Metcalf,	Levi Salisbury,
Washington "	Edwin H. Champlin,	Edwin H. Champlin,
Bristol "	John W. Dearth,	John W. Dearth,
Kent "	Torris M. Evans,	Hazard Carder.

SHERIFFS.

Newport County, Richard Shaw;
Providence County, Robert G. Lewis;
Washington County, Nathan B. Lillibridge;
Bristol County, John S. Pearce;
Kent County, Alexander Allen.

UNITED STATES CIRCUIT COURT.

B. R. CURTISS of Boston, Associate Justice of the Supreme Court of U. S.
JOHN PITMAN of Providence, District Judge.
JOHN T. PITMAN of Providence, Clerk.

CHARLES T. JAMES of Providence, Senator in Congress.
PHILIP ALLEN of Providence, Senator in Congress.
THOMAS DAVIS of North Providence, Representative from Eastern District.
BENJAMIN B. THURSTON of Hopkinton, Representative from Western District.

SAYLES, MILLER AND SIMONS, PRINTERS TO THE STATE.

CHRONOLOGICAL REGISTER.

It is not inappropriate, and I trust it will not be unacceptable, if a chronological register of some additional events, (American principally,) be appended to a document so statistical as the one now presented.

1492. America was discovered October 12th, by Christopher Columbus, a Genoese, employed in the service of Ferdinand and Isabella, of the United kingdoms of Aragon and Castile, or the kingdom of Spain; from which there was obtained for the Spanish crown, a vast increase of possessions and wealth.

1578-9. England shared largely in the riches of America, under a Patent granted by Queen Elizabeth. Also from another Patent, March 25th, 1584; a year memorable also for the establishment in Spain of the "INQUISITION."

1602. Capt. Gosnold failed to settle in New England, a country which he had at this date discovered.

1606. Virginia was divided into two Colonies, April 10th, by the order of King James, and called North and South Colony.

1607. Virginia settled by Capt. John Smith, who gave it its present name.

1620. In 1517 learning was revived in Europe, the Reformation was begun by Luther, and others in Germany, and was carried forward, particularly in England, until its final establishment by an Act of Parliament under Queen Elizabeth. On account of the great zeal of very many persons to remove from among them every vestige of popery and superstition, and to make the Bible their real rule in worship and discipline, as well as in faith, they were soon denominated by the opposing party, PURITANS, because they sought a purer church than that party thought was necessary. And the settlements of New England, in fact, were a consequence that resulted from the disputes which had attended the reformation in England. In 1608-9 several of the Puritans residing in the north of England, removed to Holland. After about twelve years residence in Leyden, the town where they had settled, they obtained a Patent of lands in this country, and soon afterwards sailed for America. They arrived at Cape Cod, on the 9th of November, 1620; bnt finding serious obstructions to their settlement there, they concluded to locate at a place called by the Indians, Patuxet; and landed the month ensuing, Dec. 22d, naming it New Plymouth. They became permanently established at Plymouth by a Patent which they had obtained "from the New England Company, the 13th of January, 1629–30." Almost all the first settlers of New England were Puritans.

1635. The First Free School in New England was founded at Charlestown, Mass.

1643. Confederation of the New England Colonies for mutual defence was formed.

1664. New York was surrendered by the Dutch to the English.

1732. George Washington was born in Westmoreland County, Virginia, February 22d.

1738. John Callender, preached his Century Sermon at Newport, March 24th.

1744. French war was began, and continued until 1748.

1754. French war was renewed—it was declared in 1756, and terminated in 1763.

1758. Newport Mercury was established June 12.

1765. Stamp Act was passed by Parliament—repealed in 1766.

1765. First Colonial Congress assembled at New York.

1767. Duties were imposed on tea, paper, glass, and painter's colors.

1773. British tea was destroyed at Boston.

1774. Boston Port Bill was passed.

1774. First Continental Congress assembled in Carpenter's Hall, in Philadelphia, on *Monday*, Sept. 5th. The session was opened with prayer by the venerable Jacob Duche, of the Protestant Episcopal Church.

1775. The first blood was shed at Lexington, Mass., on *Wednesday*, April 19th, being the commencement of the Revolutionary war. June 17th, the Battle at Breed's and Bunker Hill was fought, and Charlestown was burnt.

1775. At the Second Continental Congress, convened in New York, GEORGE

WASHINGTON, aged 43 years, was on June 15th unanimously elected by ballot, Commander-in-Chief of the American armies.

1776. THURSDAY, July 4th, Independence of the United States was declared by Congress, then in Session in Philadelphia, and *the name of* COLONIES *was blotted out forever.*

1777. Articles of Confederation were signed by the thirteen STATES.

1777. GILBERT MOTTIER LAFAYETTE of France, arrived at Charleston, South Carolina, April 25th, aged nineteen years, he having been born Sept. 6th, 1757.

1778. The Treaty of Alliance with France was made.

1780. The American Academy of Arts and Sciences was instituted.

1781. The Confederation of the States was confirmed.

1781. The Bank of North America, New York, the first American Bank, was instituted.

1782. The first seventy-four gun-ship in the United States was built at Portsmouth.

1783. Saturday, April 19th, proclamation of *Peace* with England was made at the New-Building in Philadelphia; and prayer was offered by the venerable JOHN GANO, Pastor of Gold-street Baptist Church, New York; a chaplain also in the war.

1783. Thursday, Dec. 4th, George Washington took an affectionate leave of his officers then in New York; and on Tuesday, the 23d, he resigned his commission to Congress, assembled to receive it, at Annapolis, Md.

1784. The first American voyage from New York to China was made this year.

1787. George Washington presided at the Convention to form a Constitution for the Union, which was adopted by Virginia in December, and by one State after another during years 1787–90.

1789. The Constitution of the Uuited States takes the place of the Articles of Confederation, which had been found to be in their operation weak and inefficient.

1789. George Washington at the age of fifty-six years was unanimously chosen President, and took the oath of office in New York, April 30th, it being administered to him by Chancellor Livingston. The principles of the CONSTITUTION were put into operation by Washington, and the country soon after rose from extreme depression; it has since increased in population, commerce, wealth, and power, to a degree heretofore unexampled.

1791. The first United States Bank was established in February, and its charter expired March 4th, 1811. The Providence Bank was incorporated in October, 1791.

1792. TELEGRAPH was invented by Chappe, and one was established in France in 1793, by the National Parliament.

1793. WILLAM CAREY was appointed missionary to India, Jan. 9th, and sailed from England, Thursday, June 13th.

1793. George Washington was elected for another term, March 4th. He retired to his private residence at Mt. Vernon, March 4th, 1797.

1798. Under the apprehensions of foreign aggression, Washington was elected for the second time, July 3d, Commander-in-Chief of the American army. He accepted the commission on the condition that he might select his own officers. He was not called to the field, the difficulties with France having been amicably adjusted.

1799. Previous to the reception of this adjustment, and WHILE IN COMMAND, George Washington died at his own house, at 10 1-2 o'clock, P. M., December 14th, and was burried in his own tomb on the 18th, aged sixty-seven years and ten months.

1799. The Massachusetts Missionary Society for foreign as well as home missions was organized at Boston, May 28th.

1800. The city of Washington became the seat of the general government

1800. The first Fire and Marine Insurance office was established in Rhode Island. Richard Jackson, Jr., was President from its origin until his death, which occurred on April 18th, 1838, a period of thirty-eight years.

1802. May 26th, the Massachusetts Baptist Missionary Society was organized at Boston.

1803. The Baptist Magazine was published for the first time September 1st.

1806. The Female Mite Society, of the Baptist Churches Providence, was constituted November 11th, being the first and oldest Missionary organization in Rhode Island.

1807. FULTON first uses Steamboats on the Hudson river, the first boats o their kind in America. R. Fulton died March 24th, 1815.

1808. The abolition of the slave trade was effected.

1809. Cotton Manufactories are now being multiplied; they have now become very numerous, and furnish large business for the country generally.

1810. American Board of Commissioners for Foreign Missions, was formed at Bradford, June 29th, 1810.

1810-11. Gas introduced to light streets in London, and public buildings—greatly increased in 1815.

1811. First Steamboats on the Ohio and Mississippi rivers this year.

1812. Baptist Foreign Missionary Society was organized October 14th, at Boston.

1812. Adoniram Judson, Jun., and wife were baptized at Calcutta, India, September 5th, *Lords' day*. He died at sea, April 12th, 1851.

1812. June 18th, the United States declare war against England. Treaty of Peace was concluded at Ghent, December 24th, 1814. Gen. Jackson's battle at New Orleans was fought January 8th, 1815.

1814. General Missionary Convention of the Baptist denomination in the

U. S. was organized at First Baptist Church, Philadelphia, Wednesday, May 18th.

1815. The American Education Society was instituted.

1816. The Second U. S. Bank, established April 10th. Gen. Jackson removed the deposits of the government in 1835, and the Bank ceased in a short time to exist.

1816. The American Bible Society was instituted.

1816. The Rhode Island Baptist Education Society was formed September 11th. The Massachusetts Baptist Education Society was constituted in 1814.

1819. Christian Watchman first published May 19th.

1820. JONATHAN MAXCY second President of Brown University deceased June 4th, aged 52 years. He was born September 12th, 1768. He was the same age of President Manning, his predecessor.

1820. The two hundredth anniversary of the landing of the Pilgrims at Plymouth, was celebrated at Plymouth, December 22d.

1821. Florida was ceded by Spain to the United States.

1824. The American Sunday School Union was established in Philadelphia, May 25th.

1824. Gen. Lafayette visits the United States, by invitation of President Monroe, and lands in New York in August. He was at Breeds Hill June 17th, 1825. He returned to France, Sept. 7th, 1825. His death occured at La Grange, France, May 20th, 1834.

1825. The Rhode Island Baptists State Convention was formed Thursday, August 4th.

1825. Newton Theological Institution was founded at Newton, Mass.

1825. The Erie Canal was completed.

1825. The American Temperance Society was instituted.

1827. The rails at Quincy, were the first rails laid in the United States. Railways are of ancient date. One at New Castle, in England, was constructed in 1676; and an *iron* railway was constructed at the Sheffield Colliery in 1776. An act of incorporation was granted to the Boston and Lowell Railroad Company in 1830; and also in June 1831, to each of the respective companies of the Boston and Worcester, Boston and Taunton, Boston and Providence. And subsequently to the New Bedford and Taunton, Providence and Stonington, Providence and Worcester, Fall River and Boston, Providence and Fishkill, Bristol and Providence, Newport and Fall River, which last is now in the hands of a Committee, appointed at a city gathering Dec. 17th, 1853.

1830. The Northern Baptist Education Society was formed March 24th.

1832. The American Baptist Home Missionary Society was constituted April 27th. JONATHAN GOING was its first Corresponding Secretary.

1832. The Ohio Canal was completed.

1833. The New England Sabbath School Union was established.

1836. ASA MESSER, the third President of Brown University, died at his residence in Providence, October 11th.

1837. The American and Foreign Bible Society was formed April 27th, *Thursday evening.*

1837. The great depression of Banks took place.

1843. Annals of Providence, published by W. R. STAPLES.

1846. War against Mexico was declared by the United States, March 11th. Treaty of peace was concluded February 2d, and was ratified May 30th, 1848.

1852. HENRY CLAY died at Washington June 29th.

1852. DANIEL WEBSTER, died at Marshfield, October 24th.

1853. PHILIP ALLEN, Governor of Rhode Island, was elected to the United States Senate, and was succeeded in the gubernatorial chair by FRANCIS M. DIMOND of Bristol.

1853. The loss by fire in New York from October 1, is estimated at $4,-800,000; insurance $1,730,000. Among these are the Harper's buildings, the Metropolitan Hall, and Lafarge Hotel; the latter is said to have been the finest building of the kind in the United States.

1853. The steamer San Francisco a wreck from Dec. 21st to Jan. 5th, 1854, when she sunk—200 lives lost. The GREAT REPUBLIC, the pride of its builder, the largest vessel ever constructed, in one hour was burnt level with the water.

SETTLEMENTS OF STATES.

Date.	Names.	By whom.
1607,	Virginia,	English.
1614,	New York,	Dutch.
1620,	Massachusetts,	English Puritans.
1623,	New Hampshire,	" "
1624,	New Jersey,	Dutch.
1627,	Delaware,	Sweeds and Fins.
1634,	Maryland,	Catholics.
1635,	Connecticut,	English.
1636.	Rhode Island,	R. Williams. Eng.
1650,	North Carolina,	English.
1670,	South Carolina,	" Tay Co.
1682,	Pennsylvania,	Penn.En. Quaker.
1733,	Georgia,	Gen. Oglethorpe.

The above are the original Thirteen States.

States admitted into the Union since the adoption of the Federal Constitution in 1788, settled mostly by emigrants from the other States.

1791, Vermont,	1817, Mississippi,	1837, Michigan,
1792, Kentucky,	1818, Illinois,	1845, Florida,
1796, Tennessee,	1819, Alabama,	1845, Texas,
1802, Ohio,	1820, Maine,	1846, Iowa,
1812, Louisiana,	1821, Missouri,	1848, Wisconsin,
1816, Indiana,	1836, Arkansas,	1850, California.

Presidents of Colonial Congress.

1744, Peyton Randolph,	1774, Henry Middleton.

Presidents of Continental Congress.

1775, John Hancock,	1782, Elias Boudinot,
1776, John Hancock,	1783, Thomas Mifflin,
1777, Henry Lawrens,	1784, Richard Henry Lee,
1778, John Jay,	1785, Richard Henry Lee,
1779, Samuel Huntington,	1786, Nathaniel Gorham,
1780, Thomas M'Kean,	1787, Arthur St. Clair,
1781, John Hanson,	1788, Cyrus Griffin.

Presidents of the United States.

1789, George Washington.	Retired	1797.	Deceased	Dec. 14th, 1799.
1797, John Adams.	"	1801.	"	July 4th, 1826.
1801, Thomas Jefferson.	"	1809.	"	July 4th, 1826.
1809, James Madison.	"	1817.	"	June 28th, 1836.
1817, James Monroe.	"	1825.	"	July 4th, 1831.
1825, John Quincy Adams.	"	1829.	"	Feb. 23d, 1848.
1829, Andrew Jackson.	"	1837.	"	June 8th, 1845.
1837, Martin Van Buren.	"	1841.		
1841, William Henry Harrison.			"	April 4th, 1841.
1841, John Tyler.	"	1845.		
1845, James K. Polk.	"	1849.	"	June 13th, 1849.
1849, Zachary Taylor.			"	July 10th, 1850.
1850, Millard Fillmore.	"	March 4th, 1853.		

1853, Franklin Pierce. Term expires March 4th, 1857.

1853, W. R. King, Vice President of the United States, died at his residence in Dallas Co., Alabama, April 18th, 1853.

The United States territory began to be settled in 1607, being at this date 247 years ago. The New England territory was established in 1620, two hundred and thirty-four years since; and Rhode Island in 1636, two hundred and eighteen years ago. And *July 4th*, 1854, the United States will have been a free and independent nation seventy-eight years.

The population of the United States in 1850 was, 23,263,488.

The valuation of the United States in 1850 was, $7,135,780,228.

www.ingramcontent.com/pod-product-compliance
Lightning Source LLC
LaVergne TN
LVHW021415110826
845150LV00007B/1938